THE

'GATE

Rough Badger Press

First Printing: 2017

Rough Badger Press
Denton Holme
Carlisle, Cumbria.

ISBN: 1544003366
ISBN-13: 978-1544003368

The Story of

Shaddongate United FC

JON TAIT

CONTENTS

Introduction   1
1. Carlisle Association   9
2. Red Rose   17
3. Shaddongate United   20
4. Into the New Century   27
5. When the Roses Come Again 38
6. The Ban   46
7. Carlisle United   54
8. The Lancashire Combination 64
9. The North Eastern   76
10. Money Troubles   90
11. Brunton Park   100
12. Liquidation   108
13. Rebirth   112
14. After the War   123
15. Back to the Boardroom   129
16. Champions   136
17. The English Cup   143
18. Flooded Out   151
19. The Football League   160

ACKNOWLEDGMENTS

The British Newspaper Archive's online records provided the bulk of the research for this publication. Thanks to my friends and colleagues at Royal Mail for the interest and encouragement that they have shown in the project and to my wife Sally and son Jack for all their support.

INTRODUCTION

A SO-CALLED EXPERT once called Carlisle Castle 'the ugliest in Europe.' I read it on the internet, so it must be true. The squat, square, red sandstone keep and walls might not be the prettiest but she's a functional fortress and with the Great Border City being besieged ten times, she had to be. This is the frontier land that lies just ten miles from Scotland. There are no ornate decorations to Carlisle's stronghold though there is some beautifully carved folk art on the walls of the top of the tower that was done by either bored prison guards or prisoners back in the medieval period. Graffiti, basically. But could at least some of the primitive yet striking art have been etched by an innocent man condemned to a cell that he had once guarded?

Robert Parker was jailer for the High Sherriff of Carlisle, Sir Edward Musgrave. In 1528 he took charge of notorious border reiver Richie Graham of Esk and incarcerated him in the high tower at Carlisle in shackles after he'd been captured alongside twenty-one others by the English West March Warden William Lord Dacre. Musgrave executed eight, including two of the infamous Armstrongs –widely regarded as the most lawless clan - while the rest were to be held until after the next Quarter Sessions.

Dacre planned to destroy illegally built towers in the Debateable Land but was ambushed and suspected Richie Graham of using his family connections – he was married to Armstrong of Mangerton's daughter - to warn them of the impending raid.

Although Graham was deep in trouble, his reputation provided him influence within the castle walls; the jailer James Porter refused to hand Parker the keys when he brought the prisoners from Naworth. Forget Sicily – the original mafia was formed in the Borders. Words such as blackmail, bereaved and Scott-free all originate from the area. Christopher Lowther, the castle constable, ordered the shackles removed and when the Graham's mother came to visit, took the keys from Parker and refused to give them back. When the jailer later recovered them, Lowther hit him with his dagger and threatened to stab him.

Parker complained and Graham was handed back over to be held in the castle's Sherriff prison ironed to another man until under-sheriff Sir William Musgrave ordered the chains removed. On the Sunday Graham was allowed to hear mass in the chapel and dine in the hall while his brother, John, 'The Brade,' spent an hour with Lowther in the castle earlier that day.

Parker was taking Graham back to his cell when a man named Thomas Wright distracted him. Graham said he wanted to go the privy postern gate and while Parker searched for his keys, he speared it shut. But Graham clambered over and an accomplice was waiting with a horse in the fields below to make their

escape.

Parker called on several people to help him, including one Robert Storey, but was ignored. Although he went after Graham on horseback, no-one joined the pursuit.

The whole episode stinks of a set-up.

Sir Edward Musgrave was implicated with Sir William Musgrave, Christopher Lowther, Parker and Robert Robson, keeper of the postern gate keys – who'd been forbidden to lock up by Lowther on the day - as accomplices, though only Parker was accused by the Cumberland gentry on the inquest panel.

What happened to Parker isn't recorded. However, if one speculates that the High Tower in Carlisle was at the top of the keep – where the carvings are located – it is possible that he was incarcerated there himself. Maybe we'll never know. But history does provide some answers. It was in fact the Storeys that had betrayed Dacre's raid, not Richie Graham. They fled their land on Esk and set up in north Northumberland to escape retribution from both Dacre and the Grahams. That severely implicates the Robert Storey in Carlisle Castle. The Grahams crossed the border under the protection of the Scottish West March Warden Lord Maxwell until things settled down then returned to divide up the Storey's land.

By 1529 Christopher Dacre had taken the role of High Sheriff of Carlisle from Edward Musgrave. Cardinal Thomas Wolsey ordered Thomas Musgrave to hand over Bewcastle castle to Dacre, but found that he'd stripped the lead, smashed the windows and left it uninhabitable.

The carvings that visitors to the castle now ponder over feature animals, religious scenes, knights and heraldic crests and Carlisle builder Mike Parker knows all about the stonemasonry required to carve so intricately into sandstone.

"It takes a huge amount of skill and patience to do work like that, even today," he said. Just a careless chip of the chisel and it's ruined.

One of the most prominent carvings your eyes settle upon through the toughened glass that protects them features a stag's head by a crescent moon. The family crest of the Parkers, who were landowners at Petterill Green, features buck's heads and crescents. Though the Parkers have long been in Cumbria, the story began unravelling when Mike said he was unsure if he could be descended for Robert the jailer.

"I'm not sure if I'm related to the Parkers who were in the City then, but my family have been in the area for a long time," he said, and went back to coaching his Denton Holme boys under-sevens football side in the sun.

One thing that's certain is that Robert Parker was a pawn in a power struggle between two influential families and it's not impossible is that could have left his tale in stone, in coded messages to be unraveled or lost in time; the guard who became a prisoner.

The experts at English Heritage seem to think it unlikely though, as they didn't respond to the requests for comment from the bearded sports hack in a leather jacket.

So the Castle clings to its secrets; the mysteries that could have been solved if someone had just chiseled 'woz 'ere.' But then maybe some things are just better left that way. Omerta maintains a grip at Carlisle even today.

The rugged, upland, rural county of Cumberland is probably better known for wresting, fell running and sausages than soccer. However, one of the first ever recorded international football fixtures took place in the county back in the days of the reivers. The lawless clans that lived on either side of the dividing line between England and Scotland from the 1400s until the mid-1600s loved their horse racing and their football – or as it was simply known back then, the baa'. Clan chieftains arranged games as a pretext for gathering their followers for a raid on their neighbours which could see them hit a single farm or an entire town, burning, looting and fighting.

It was a team of twelve of the Scottish Armstrong's of Liddesdale that came to Bewcastle to play a game against a dozen local English lads in May 1599. They took off their steel Spanish burgonet helmets and removed their swords before taking to the pitch, no doubt confident in their sporting abilities as the Scottish side were all notorious riders. So notorious, in fact, that when the English authorities heard about the game, they planned to take them in a surprise attack to save them the danger of riding into Liddesdale to try and apprehend them.

The Armstrong's were tipped off about the ambush though, and when six of them went to the local pub for a few pints with the locals after the match, they had two hundred of their mates waiting to pounce on the English when they went to spring their 'surprise' attack.

William Ridley and Nicholas Welton had their throats cut, a Robson was also killed and a man named John Whitfield's guts spilled out after he was slashed in the belly while the Scots also took thirty prisoners. It's not known if they tore up the pitch and smashed the goalposts like their ancestors in the Tartan Army did at Wembley in the 1970s.

Mary Queen of Scots watched a couple of matches being played by twenty members of her retinue on Bitts Park by the broad, slow moving river Eden behind Carlisle Castle where she was being held under house arrest in 1568, and a small stitched leather ball from the time was discovered in Mary's bed chamber at Stirling Castle in the 1970s by workers removing oak panelling.

Her lover James Hepburn, the Earl of Bothwell, also enjoyed a game but he had a bit of a temper on him and when he took a knock from another player he turned around and booted him back, which led to a punch up and demands for a duel that King James VI had to put a stop to. Bothwell fancied himself as a bit of a dandy, a hipster-type character, and he was lucky not to get killed by a reiver. 'Wha dair meddle wi me?' is the famous line associated with the Scottish West March raider Jock Elliot in a Border Ballard written about the notorious bad man. It was more than just boasting and bragging. Jock was an evil little scrapper with a hot temper and a sharp blade in an area filled with hooligans. Hepburn went to capture Elliot for his crimes and knocked him from his horse. But the aristocrat made the mistake of going over to check the body of Little Jock of the Park, who was lying flat out on the ground. As Hepburn went to turn him over, Elliot produced a knife and stabbed him several times. The Queen raced from Edinburgh on horseback to see her badly injured beau, was hurt in a fall, took ill from the wet Border weather and almost died herself.

Carlisle Castle was also used as the prison to detain the notorious Kinmont Willie Armstrong, a noted reiver who was wanted for numerous crimes by the English. His clan were noted for their ability to put upwards of three thousand men in the saddle for a raid so he must he been a formidable fighter and noted hard-man as well as a famous thief. Kinmont's capture by English riders on a day of truce was a scandal of the day. He was riding home along the Eden riverbank and the temptation proved too much for a gang of English riders on the other side of the water who splashed across and captured the Scottish reiver. Armstrong should have been protected by the terms of the truce day, which gave free passage to and from the meeting, but was bound in chains and locked up in the castle, which infuriated Sir Walter Scott of Buccleuch. Scott was the Keeper of Liddesdale, the bloodiest valley in the Borders and home to the Armstrong and Elliot clans. His crowning glory came in 1596 when he organised the breakout of captured Kinmont from the Castle. It was a daring and ambitious raid that caused the English much embarrassment. When he was summoned in front of Queen Elizabeth to answer for his actions, his is reputed to have answered: "What is it that a man dare not do," which so impressed her that she told her courtiers that with ten thousand men like him, Scotland could 'shake the firmest throne of Europe.' Scott was also involved in personal vendettas against the Charlton's in Northumberland and regularly led huge raids into Tynedale to cause much disruption by firing homes, murdering people and lifting cattle. Despite the carnage, The Bold Buccleuch was also a ranking member of the establishment.

The capture and subsequent breakout of Kinmont Willie are celebrated today in mosaic on a couple of walls on the underpass of the nearby Hardwicke Circus roundabout in the shadow of the City Council offices. Now there's an ugly building. The reivers would have delighted in firing it, their surnames now all etched in the underpass from the Tullie House museum to the Castle by the 'cursing stone,' a block of granite inscribed with a curse imposed on them by the Archbishop of Glasgow. These violent men were the forerunners of the game in the area.

A mosaic of the captured Kinmont Willie Armstrong at Carlisle.

1. CARLISLE ASSOCIATION

I T'S SOMEWHAT TRICKY pinning down the early roots of football in Carlisle because although Carlisle Football Club is mentioned prominently in records back in 1884, the year that the Cumberland Football Association was formed, that side was in fact a rugby club. When you throw in the problem that the 'football' fixtures at the time mix in both the handling and the kicking game, it all gets a bit confusing. Well for a daft Geordie like me, anyway. The north east never really embraced the Union code like north Cumbria did then, and out West they loved the League version of the sport. When you consider that the rugby and football clubs tended to share grounds, then it gets even more tangled.

The magic words 'Association Football' first really appear around 1886, with the Carlisle Association Club being the main side in the City, though a report in the *Bolton Evening News* in 1905 said that Carlisle was the oldest Association Club in Cumberland and was formed in 1878. So there you go.

Carlisle had boomed with the arrival of cotton

mills during the Industrial Revolution as the red brick terraces and cobbled streets of Denton Holme and Caldewgate spilled from outside the old West Walls of the medieval city to house an ever-growing population of former farm labourers that arrived from the surrounding countryside. Carlisle was so crowded in the old tenements in the Lanes of the old City Centre that riots were commonplace, as was disease, with people packed into filthy conditions with open sewers alongside butcher's shops. The City was growing; a canal was run from Shaddongate to Port Carlisle to link Carlisle with the major trading port of Liverpool, then the railways arrived and were a great boon to the town. The railroad yards at Kingmoor were at one time the biggest in Europe.

Carlisle Association Football Club was being described as of old standing and being the 'parent of the other combinations in the City' in 1888, so they'd definitely been formed earlier than that date. One of the early Carlisle sides played at Cemetery Lane where they drew 1-1 with Wigton in 1886, and lined up as follows - Carlisle: R. Bell, goal, I. Graham and D.E. Straiton, backs, I. Potts, W. Rome, and W. Bell, half backs, J. Gibson (Captain), E. Gibson, W. Newcombe, H. Ivison and W. Nott, forwards. Their umpire was Mr. W.H. Reed. Ivison headed against the bar before Wigton went ahead with a soft shot that beat the goalkeeper, but Carlisle levelled shortly after when J. Gibson crossed for Newcombe who 'cleverly headed it through.' Both sides were praised in the report for the smartness of their passing. Newcombe was a fast player; the report reckoned he could sacrifice a little of his speed for more accuracy, while E. Gibson 'as usual, tried to do too much work' and was often 'wandering from his left wing position to the right.' Straiton played well and must have just signed as

Carlisle felt he could be a good acquisition for the club. For the record, the Wigton team lined up with J. Davidson in goal, the backs were R. Scott and W. Young; W. Hammel, G. Mattison and F. Dixon the half backs while the forward line was T. Johnstone (Captain), J. Robinson, T. Robinson, J. Moore and W. King. Mr. J. Pennington was their umpire and the match was refereed by Mr. Plucknett.

At the end of the 1887/88 season the club had played 18 matches and won nine, lost eight and drew one, against Annan, with 48 goals scored by Carlisle and 50 conceded. There were a few more details at the end of the 1888/89 season with Carlisle playing 28, winning sixteen, losing nine and drawing three. The team that drew 2-2 with Eaglesfield towards the end of the season lined up - *Carlisle:* J. Aston, goal; A. J. Thomas and J.C. Graham, backs; H. Ivison, E. Gibson and G. Carruthers, half backs; J. Gibson, T.H. Hodgkinson, G. Jardine, R.R. Wilson and T. Carr, forwards.

The sides that Carlisle won against were Nithsdale (Dumfries), Keswick, Dalston, Aspatria Agricultural College, Glasgow College, Canonbie, Annan, Appleby and Midgeholme. They drew with Eaglesfield, Moffat and Appleby and the defeats were inflicted by Millom (in a cup tie), mid-Annandale, Nithsdale, Hamilton Academicals, Sunderland Albion, Canonbie, Keswick, Annan and Wigton.

The honorary secretary of the club was Mr. George N. Beattie, who was negotiating with the big sides Queen's Park and Preston North End for games the following season, where games had already been arranged against the likes of Sunderland Albion, Newcastle East End and Queen of the South Wanderers.

Carlisle Association weren't just happy to play

against the local Cumbrian sides but were casting a wider, more ambitious net to take on the established Scottish, north-east and Lancashire teams as well. Although the Association game had been mainly started by public schoolboys returning to their towns and bringing the game back with them, Carlisle Association seem to have been an original working-class side with the players coming from the local community.

In 1890 the Carlisle Association Club were playing at Waterworks Lane, while the Carlisle Rugby Club had a pitch on Lismore Place between Warwick Road and Victoria Place. The site was probably near where the Carlisle Youth Zone buildings now stand, with the roofs and floodlights of the current Brunton Park clearly visible across the fields of Newman school.

Cummersdale Hornets were now playing on the Cemetery Lane ground and South Vale Wanderers were at Willow Holme. Other Carlisle teams in 1890 included West End, Signal Works Rovers (who played at Currock Road), Carlisle Trinity (who played at Raffles), Stanwix, Scotby and Gas Works Rovers, who played at Bousteads Grassing, though these appear to have been predominantly rugby sides rather than strictly playing the association code.

In the February of 1890 the seeds of dissention between the Carlisle side and local football's governing body, the Cumberland FA, who were, and still are based in Workington, began to be sown after a disputed Cumberland Association Challenge Cup second round tie between Carlisle Association and Arlecdon. The tiny village side from near Whitehaven in Copeland complained before kick-off that two of the Carlisle players – Ross and Jardine – weren't bona fide members of the club.

It was a rough game in front of a large crowd at the

Arlecdon ground. One of the village defenders was cautioned for fouling Thomas, who had been displaying some nice dribbling skills. After forcing four corners, Arlecdon went ahead as Sables got the ball past Carlisle keeper Hunt. In the second half, Thomas embarked on another run and fired a shot against the bar, which fell kindly for Powell who put it away during a 'scrimmage' in which blows were taken and handed out. Carlisle's Ross and Arlecdon keeper Watson were both sent off. With no further goals, Carlisle refused to play extra time so the villagers claimed the win, with the matter being referred to the Cumberland FA. Carlisle's team for the tie was: A.G.S. Hunt, goal; T. Carr and D.E. Straiton, backs; H. Ivison, A.E. Gibson and H.J. Pilmer, half backs; A.J. Thomas (captain), G. Jardine, R.W. Ross, W. Forsythe and O.U. Powell, forwards. The game was refereed by Mr. Rich of Askam.

When the game was replayed at Wigton, a further dispute erupted over a disallowed Carlisle goal. With the matter up in front of the Association with the president Rev. W.G.C. Hodgson in the chair, Carlisle's protest was that a goal scored by Aston was not allowed. The referee, Mr. Rich, wrote in that 'in his opinion the ball did not go over the line.' Carlisle secretary Mr. Beattie took a much different view, however, and maintained that the ball was in and the referee and umpires weren't close enough to see it. Mr. Dixon, the Arlecdon representative, protested that Carlisle didn't claim the goal until the end of the match with the referee's letter backing this up. The game was ordered to be replayed again at Arlecdon, with Mr. Beattie's request that it be played at Maryport or Workington being defeated in a vote. Clearly upset at the events, he said: "I think it will come to this, that Carlisle will refuse to play. It seems that the West will 'do' Carlisle out of the Cup if they possibly can."

Carlisle had a strong side; they'd thumped Appleby 8-2 in a game around the time with Thomas, Powell and Brough all scoring twice and Ivison and Forsythe adding the others. The team that day was Hamilton, goal; Carr and Clarke, backs; Ivison, Pilmer and Donnan, half backs; Thomas (captain), Ross, Brough, Forsythe and Powell, forwards.

Early in the September of 1890 the ambitious Carlisle Association Club opened their new ground behind Brunton Place, known as the Borough Grounds, which the committee had leased from Mr. Spottiswood of the Beehive, firmly placing a date on when football first started to be played around the area of the modern day stadium. Carlisle had been accepted as members of the English Association and the following month they played against Bootle in the first qualifying round of the English Cup (now, of course, the FA Cup). They went down 6-1 at the Borough Grounds, with Forsythe netting the only goal after Jamieson, Grierson, Murray, Deans and Orr (2) had put the visitors in charge, but the season was to prove a success with Carlisle reaching the final of the Cumberland Cup, going down 2-0 against Workington at Maryport. Carlisle were pleased not only in the better standard of their play, but also in the increasing attendances at their games. They had played 37 games and won 26, lost six and drawn five with a bumper haul of 149 goals being scored and 55 conceded. The gate money was on the up, too. In 1887 the highest take through the turnstiles was 16s 6d. In 1888, £2 19s 10d and in 1889, when they'd hosted Blackburn Rovers at the Lismore Place ground kindly lent by the Carlisle Rugby Football Club, they'd taken a healthy £27. Carlisle were clearly the premier association football club in the City.

But all of that hope and optimism came crashing down and by June 1891 the club's annual general meeting at the Albert Hotel was adjourned sine die as only five members bothered to turn up. The club were £60 in debt, with £15 being owed to the secretary Mr. Beattie, and no games had yet been arranged for the following season.

Carlisle Association appeared to be all but finished. But what had gone so badly wrong? The club had arranged a Grand Evening Concert in the County Hotel in the March, but the turnout was described as 'disheartening' and 'extremely meagre' and while further details have proved difficult to find, there clearly had been a fall out of some description among the members of the club.

CARLISLE ASSOCIATION FOOTBALL CLUB.—The third annual meeting of this club was held at the Prince of Wales Hotel, Denton Holme, on Thursday evening, Sept. 15th., when the committee and officers were elected for ensuing season: with Mr. H. Hartley as captain, and Mr. R. Barnes, secretary. In consequence of the rapid spread of the Association Game in this district, the secretary announced that he had been enabled to prepare an excellent programme of matches.

The Third AGM of the Carlisle Association Club at the Prince of Wales in Denton Holme in September 1881. That confirms the year of the formation of Association football in Carlisle as 1878.

A Cumberland County team in 1897. The moustachioed W. Ross, of Carlisle Association, is sat second in from the right and scored with a shot in off the post during a 4-2 Cumberland Cup Final defeat by Workington in April that year. There was trouble after the game with sods and stones being thrown.

2. RED ROSE

IN 1892, CARLISLE RED ROSE were in the draw to play in the Cumberland Football Association Shield. With no other Carlisle sides in the hat, it can only be assumed that the Rose, as they became known, had taken up the baton for the Association game in the City. D. Bunting and R. Hayes were the club's delegates at the Cumberland FA Annual Meeting in August as they were admitted as a new club.

In December of that year, Red Rose were beaten 5-3 by Workington Black Diamonds in a reply the semi-finals of the competition, with Johnstone netting twice and the other being headed into his own goal by a Black Diamonds player.

The Rose were playing at Cemetery Lane (probably around the vicinity of Richardson Street in Denton Holme today, since Cummersdale Hornets rugby side were also using the ground) and beat the County Cup holders Moss Bay Exchange 5-1 in front of a large number of spectators. Monk, McKinley, B. Johnston (2) and Underwood chalked up the goals.

The other clubs in membership of the CFA at the

time were Dalston, Wigton Harriers and Aspatria; Maryport (Grasslot), Cockermouth, Keswick and Braithwaite; Workington, Black Diamonds, Chapelbank Rovers, Mossbay Exchange and Old St. Michaels; Frizington (White Star), Winder Rangers, Frizington Rovers, Arlecdon and St. Pauls (Frizington).

The Red Rose players A. Carruthers (right back), W. McKillop, a right half back who also had the distinction of being the captain, and the centre half back R. Underwood played in a Cumberland v Northumberland Juniors select side in January 1893.

However, in January 1895, the following Carlisle City players were appearing for Cumberland in a 7-4 win over Northumberland at the Borough Grounds – H. Brown, H. Ivison and W. Ross. The Northumberland team contained players from Newcastle United, Shankhouse, Trafalgar, Blyth, Rendel and Hexham Excelsior.

And in September 1895, the Carlisle City Association Football Club opened their new season with a 2-1 win over Appleby at the Borough Grounds, so it certainly appears that the old Carlisle Association side was back with a new name. The familiar names of H. Ivison and W. Ross, along with H. Brown were again selected as 'Carlisle' players to appear for Cumberland against Cleveland at Darlington that month and in November Carlisle Association faced Hexham Excelsior at the Borough Grounds. A team called Carlisle Albion were playing Annan Border in an Association game at Harraby the same day. Carlisle also appears to have had a reserve team and Carlisle N.E.R had a side, presumably made up of railway workers. The Carlisle Association side that beat Black Diamonds 2-1 in a Cumberland League game around the time lined up – *Carlisle Association*: Kinghorn: H. Brown and Moses: McKillop, Ivison and Conway;

Forsyth, Tinkler, Ellis, W. Ross and Bulman. The players T.H. Hodgkinson, W.S. Graham and J. Bell were away on County duty in a match that Cumberland lost 7-5 against Lancashire on the Warwick Road Ground in Carlisle on the same day.

On Christmas Day, Carlisle Association acquitted themselves well against the 5th K.R.V. from Dumfries, a team that had beaten them 9-2 some time ago, had lost two or three regular players and drew some from their second team. They played Distington on Boxing Day, but the game was so drab that the reporter reckoned it didn't call for much comment. Two months later the *Lancashire Evening Post* was reporting that the heavy frost and snow had wiped out the Carlisle fixtures but also interestingly noted that the Carlisle Association were billed to play against Moss Bay in the County Cup – the clubs two clubs *being the finalists for the trophy the previous year*. The Carlisle side had 'pluckily lifted the trophy' then, so Carlisle Association must have been reformed around 1894, perhaps re-taking the reigns from Red Rose. It's all very tangled and confusing. Not to mention the bloody rugby, which was at least referred to as Rugby Football in the records by this time, thereby eradicating some of the perplexity. In the April, Carlisle Association 'added another win to their already long list of successes' by beating Middlesbrough Grange 3-2. Carlisle's Rugby side suffered a tragedy in 1896 when the popular player Bell received a serious head injury in a Cumberland County game against Yorkshire at Workington and was rushed to the Cumberland Infirmary, but died later at his home as a result of the accident. Red Rose received no further mention in the press again until 1897, when they were beaten 2-1 by Newcastleton at Harraby, with Parker scoring the goal.

3. SHADDONGATE UNITED

S OMETHING MAGICAL happens to Carlisle at
dusk; the receding low sun illuminating the
red brick and sandstone buildings of the City
in a warm glow comforting as the smell of baking
biscuits from the McVitie's factory that drifts across
the wet slate roofs of Shaddongate today.

Shaddongate Mill was built during the years of
1835 and 36 and has now been converted into luxury
apartments but it's the huge Dixon's chimney that
towers above the former cotton factory that
dominates the skyline west of the old City walls. The
chimney was originally 300 feet high but had ten foot
removed during the 1970s and marks the former
industrial heart of the town, with old mills and textile
factories spread out along the river Caldew through
Denton Holme and down to Cummersdale.

It was from among this sprawl of factories and
warehouses that Shaddongate United were formed in
around 1896 and they were the Carlisle Association
Charity Shield winners that year, when the
newspapers reckoned that the 'newly-formed' Red

Rose club 'would be a trifle hard to shake off this season.' Surely that should be re-formed? But whatever the case, in the January of 1897, the two clubs did indeed meet at the Borough Grounds in the semi-finals of the competition and the Rose ran out 3-2 winners with goals from Parker and Wilkinson, who bagged a brace, while United's goalscorers were Martin and Geordie Stubbs. Shaddongate turned the tables in the March when they beat Red Rose 3-2 in a local derby at Harraby.

Shaddongate, who played at Willow Holme, were 4-1 victors over Annan in November but went out of the Cumberland Association Shield 4-3 at Wigton Harriers. G. Stubbs and Jackson got on the scoresheet, with the third coming from a penalty and the scorer not being recorded for posterity.

In December, the senior club in the City, Carlisle Association, played their first game against the Shaddongate side with the game 'arousing a lot of interest among followers of socker (sic) football in Carlisle.' In fact, when the Shaddongate club sent out their challenge to the old established side, they 'were inclined to think the junior combination were a little too presumptuous.' United pressed their challenge and Carlisle Association eventually accepted with the proceeds from the gate to go towards the funds of the locked-out engineers in the town.

The report on the game said that The 'Gate' had 'given a much better exhibition of the association game (considering they were handicapped in weight) than it has been the pleasure of Carlisle spectators to see for some time.' Carlisle had most of the pressure, but the game ended in a creditable 2-2 draw and the reporter reckoned that Shaddongate 'might do worse than to go in for the Cumberland Cup next season.' The side were clearly seen as minor upstarts by the slightly patronising tone of the piece which was probably written by a Carlisle Association official, as was customary at the time. Barnfather and Fullen put United two up, but the City hit back with goals from Kearns and Yates. Earlier in the year, Carlisle centre forward Ellis had been away down to Burnley for a month's trial; the reporter felt that he didn't have much skill and was an erratic player and Ellis was 'reckoned as anything but a strong spot in the Carlisle team.' Maybe the writer fancied a shot in the League himself.

That November had seen the sad death of a Workington player which led to a coroner's enquiry and allegations of manslaughter. John Robert Fisher, an ironworker, had been playing for the Reds in the County Association Challenge Cup Final played at the Carlisle Rugby Club's ground on Warwick Road back in the March and there'd been a riot at the end after Workington had beaten Carlisle 4-2. When the Workington players were leaving the ground they were pelted with sods of earth and rocks. A stone hit Fisher on the temple and 'knocked him insensible.' The report described how 'there had been a most brutal exhibition of rowdyism on the part of the spectators. There were not one or two solitary cases, but a sort of mob riot.' Fisher was a popular member of the Workington team and was a clever and promising player. He'd been bedridden for nineteen weeks following the blow and his death caused a lot of pain and anger, his team-mates wearing black badges for their game against Mickley on hearing of his passing.

The same month saw two Arlecdon players charged with assaulting a referee in a Shield game against Cockermouth. When the ref cautioned Tyson Frost, a 19 year old labourer, for using bad language, the player said: "I'll kick their ******* guts out!" referring to the opposition team. He also threatened to 'knock the ref's neck out' and punched him in the guts and mouth. The ref stopped the game and went to escape in the Sun Inn, but 18-year-old John Baker, also a labourer, came up and whacked him on the back of the head from behind. The Arlecdon spectators had encouraged them. Both Frost and Baker had to pay a £5 fine or face a month's hard labour in jail and were suspended indefinitely, while the Arlecdon ground was closed until the end of the year. The chairman of the bench stated that: 'Football was one of the finest English games, but the conduct of young ruffians like the defendants made respectable people keep away from the matches.' The game has had its problems from the very start.

Things were at least going well on the pitch in Carlisle; in the February of 1899, Shield holders Shaddongate had beaten Keswick 2-1 at Carlisle but went down 3-1 in the return under the looming presence of Skiddaw. Barnfather put the Gate ahead shortly before half time but goals from Litt (2) and Shearman, amid great applause, turned the game on its head.

And the footballing dynasty in Carlisle would be changed forever in September 1899 when the Carlisle Association Club, the oldest and most senior side in the City, folded. The side had had many ups and downs in its history but was now extinct altogether. There were only one or two people interested in its management the previous season and 'they'd received such meagre support that they were only too glad to get all responsibility off their hands.'

Shaddongate United were said to have 'sprung rapidly a good position, and have record of which they may well feel proud. Their prospects for the incoming season are most encouraging. Their secretary has already excellent list of fixtures arranged, including all the chief Cumberland teams and the South of Scotland clubs.'

Motherwell had travelled down to play against United the previous year and there was a probability that Shaddongate would return the favour, with a tour of Scotland being muted at the time. The club was entered for the Cumberland Cup and had two junior teams entered for the Cumberland Shield.

The newspapers noted that 'the club has been wise in the choice of their captain with Keddy being again established in that honourable position. All the old team will be available except the redoubtable 'Sammy' Fallen, who has gone to Edinburgh. But Hutton, late of the City, has joined the club and can well take Sammy's position at outside left.'

United had several new players to choose from and their forward line was 'without doubt the fastest set in Cumberland, being composed of both amateur and professional sprinters; and a little strengthening of their back division may bring the United to a proud position the Association game.' Annan were also expected to provide some assistance with players.

The Red Rose were to continue playing at Maryport Cottages, and had high hopes of a successful season. They had also arranged a good list of fixtures while Kennedy had been selected as captain – 'and a good one he will make.' The Rose were entering for the Cumberland Cup, and had all their old players available plus three of the defunct Carlisle City side had joined them. Red Rose had been finalists for the Cumberland Shield the previous year.

The City field in Melbourne Park had been taken on by the railroad workers of the Midland club and 'other junior clubs are also reported be doing well, and their players are all anxious for the fray.' The balance of power in the City was shifting and a twelve goal blitz of Newbie Engineers from Annan with almost every player getting on the scoresheet showed just how strong the Gate had become; both Red Rose and United had been admitted to the Cumberland Senior League in the August of 1899 and when they met in November the match had to be abandoned due to torrential downpours with the Gate 1-0 up at the time.

New sides Aspatria Agricultural College, the Carlisle Trading Company eleven (a Thursday side) and St. Bees were all affiliated to the CFA as the Association game continued to grow in popularity. Cummersdale Hornets, who had been a rugby side, were now also playing with a round ball as a number of rugby clubs began to embrace the other sport.

Cup holders Shaddongate had been five goals down at Workington when a tie was abandoned due to the weather and they didn't bother going to the coast to play the final fifteen minutes, reckoning it would be impossible to net six times, so the Seasiders, as they were known in the press at the time, advanced into the semi-finals.

In December, Shaddongate were bottom of the League, having lost all four of their games 2-1. Black Diamonds topped the table, with Moss Bay Exchange, Workington, Frizington White Star and Carlisle Red Rose occupying the other positions in the Senior League of just six clubs. There were, however, a lot of club games (friendlies) and Cup ties being played. Red Rose had made the Final of the Cumberland Shield against White Star. The Rose were said to be 'exhibiting form far above that expected of a junior team, and by beating Workington the other Saturday in the Senior League proved what they can do when on their mettle.' A keen struggle between East and West was expected.

Despite the hit and miss start, Shaddongate thrashed Workington 11-0 in the second round of the Cumberland Shield with Elliot, Straughton and Dalton on target in the first half before an absolute demolition job after the turnaround.

Shaddongate had also gone to Cummersdale Hornets and beaten them 3-0 with goals from Stubbs (2) and Barnfather. Full back Campbell, 'Tot' Burgess, Keddy and Geordie Stubbs all played well for the Gate with Harkness and Watson defending gamely for the village side. Warwick and Eddy did well down the left but Cummersdale missed their defender Rogerson, who was absent. Other local clubs playing games in 1899 included Midland Loco, Wigton Harriers, Dalston Black Reds and Longtown. The two latter sides played out a draw in a friendly at Dalston on the same day with Hope shooting the 'Langtooners' ahead and W. Walton levelling from a Ruddick centre.

Just before Christmas a Carlisle and District Eleven took on Shaddongate United at the Willow Holme ground in aid of the County's Transvaal War Fund and the Border City was noted as being 'a veritable nursery for Association Football.' A number of players from the defunct Carlisle City club were reputed to be thinking of 'throwing in their lot with a certain City club,' which must have been the whisper among the crowd at the game. That club was Red Rose, rather than Shaddongate.

4. INTO THE NEW CENTURY

THERE IS AN industrial estate at Willow Holme now, but a football pitch still exists beside a bus depot and behind a vast Sainsbury's superstore with a smattering of trees alongside that is owned and maintained by the City Council.

One can only imagine the lines of men in cloth caps with a cloud of cigarette smoke billowing behind them as them made their way down to the ground on a wet day in their macs back in 1900. When Shaddongate scored a disputed second goal during a goalmouth scramble in a game against Moss Bay Exchange in the March of that year, it was indignantly protested by the visiting players and the reporter reckoned that even the Gate fans muttered that it wasn't a goal in a quieter manner. It was enough to put them into the semi-finals of the Cumberland Cup against Workington Reds, though, so no-one was complaining too much. United were still bottom of the Cumberland Senior League having won just one and losing six of their eight fixtures, with 12 goals for and 15 against.

Red Rose had played 5, won two and lost three with just eight goals for and only six against. Black Diamonds topped the table.

Red Rose played a friendly against Cummersdale Hornets at Maryport Cottages and it was interesting to note that three of their players – Stainton, Johnston and O'Hara were away assisting Midland Loco in their Cup tie on the same day. Kinghorn, the old Carlisle City goalkeeper, did well for the Rose and made some great saves. Noble, Groggins, Kennedy and Irving all played good games for the hosts with Robinson also doing well in the nets for the Hornets. The newspaper questioned if it was in the side's best interests to split up the team as they had and asked – 'Did they want the Rose to wilt?'

For the following season, 1900/01, interest in the game continued to grow and the Cumberland Senior League was expanded to comprise of Shaddongate United, Red Rose, Frizington White Star, Black Diamond, Keekle, Cockermouth Crusaders, Workington, Moss Bay Exchange, Wigton Harriers, Keswick and West Seaton Rangers.

A 5-1 victory over Eamont Rovers put Shaddongate through in the Cumberland Shield for a visit to their rivals Red Rose at Maryport Cottages. The Rose had enjoyed a storming start to the campaign by winning their opening three games, scoring 12 and conceding just once, so their confidence was high. United had won one and lost two, scoring six and conceding 12 at the other end.

In December, United went down 3-1 at Keswick's Greta Grove ground with the home side's Shearman – reckoned to be 'the best all-round man in Cumberland' – grabbing a hat-trick. Keswick's speedy left-winger Hately broke his leg just above the ankle during the fixture. United were up to third in the table behind the Black Diamonds and Frizington White Star, with four wins and three defeats while the Rose, who had been involved in a string of Cup ties, drew 2-2 with Cockermouth Crusaders in the Cumberland Shield Final.

United had an Irish junior International in their ranks at the time called Cuthbertson, and he performed well along with Campbell and Spottiswoode in a 2-0 win at Wigton Harriers' Highmoor Park to inflict an eighth defeat of the season on the home side. A report stated that 'time had not long passed since the Harriers considered Shaddongate only good enough for the second team, but the tables have been turned since then with a vengeance.' United were clearly on the up but this was still very much the local game; Workington were playing in the English Cup and had ambitions of progressing further while the likes of United and Red Rose were just making the transition up from the minor ranks into the senior county game.

Shaddongate came from behind as they were beaten 3-2 at Frizington White Star in the first leg of the semi-finals of the Cumberland Cup with Spottiswood and Stubbs on target after C. Riley had scored twice, one a penalty, and his brother had added the other in the first half. In the return leg at Willow Holme Shaddongate won 2-1 and, with the away goals rule not being introduced at the time, the two clubs had to meet for a third time to settle the matter on a neutral ground.

Although they continued their good form into the League with a 4-2 victory at Cockermouth Crusaders, Shaddongate then crashed 3-1 at Red Rose with the semi-final replay possibly in the back of their minds. It took Frizington just five minutes to open the scoring in front of a good crowd at Workington's

Ashfield Ground but United pressed continually after that. They got their reward in the second half as goals from Barnfather, Stubbs and Spottiswood saw them through.

United players J. Johnston, Campbell and J. Graham were being capped by the County in a game against Liverpool at the time and were the only Carlisle players in the side captained by Workington's E. Swift. But it wasn't all plain sailing and Shaddongate had to sweat it out after Frizington, the Cup holders, put in a protest about the Cumberland Cup replay by claiming that F.F. Burgess was an ineligible player but had no evidence and United could prove that he'd played for them in games against Annan, Haltwhistle and Newcastleton that season so the protest was thrown out. Interestingly, Burgess was listed on the team sheet as 'Ruddick' for 'family reasons' which had been explained for the Association beforehand, but still raises a few questions today. Suspicions were raised that all of the games that he'd appeared in had been played outside the County and the 'Gate also had a well-known player of the same surname – 'Tot' Burgess. Red Rose were also in hot water and were suspended until 48 hours after they'd paid off a debt of 16s 6d owed to the White Star club who were clearly in a huff.

Shaddongate played out a couple of drawn games with Cummersdale Hornets, the first winners of the Carlisle & District League that season, in the Carlisle Charity Shield then beat Wigton Harriers 3-0 in the Cumberland Senior League. The Cumberland Cup had been won twice by Carlisle Association, nine times by Workington, two times by Moss Bay and twice by Black Diamonds since its inception in 1885 so it came as a bit of a surprise when Shaddongate took the trophy with a 3-1 win over Workington in front of a crowd of 1,500 at Keswick.

The reputed 'ringer' F.F. Burgess opened the scoring on a bumpy ground with a penalty after just ten minutes and Keddy made it two when he got on the end of a free kick three minutes before the break. When Workington pressed immediately from the restart, Shaddongate broke and added a killer third. Smith pulled one back for Reds with twenty minutes to go but the Carlisle side were triumphant and were greeted by a large crowd and much rejoicing on their return to the Great Border City. They'd also lifted the Carlisle and District Shield to complete a double.

West Cumberland was very much seen as the hot-bed of Association football in the County and Workington had reached the third round of the English Cup qualifying rounds that season before being knocked out by Southport Central. The Reds were keen to make a further impression on the game and were considering a move into the Lancashire League, to whom they'd applied before unsuccessfully.

Cockermouth Crusdaders had beaten Red Rose (finalists for the third successive season) in the Cumberland Shield, so it was with some consternation that the West clubs looked on as the trophies went East. But more seriously for Red Rose, who had been in the running for the County League championship, the club had run into financial difficulties and it was being reported that 'it was now doubtful if the club will again be resuscitated, in its present form and name, at any rate.'

With the first senior silverware in the bag, Shaddongate went into the 1901/02 season in a confident mood although they'd lost Hughie Campbell, who signed for Workington to play in the Lancashire League with their application this time proving a hit. The probable side for the campaign was

Smith, T. Longrigg and J. Johnston, W. Graham (captain), F. Stubbs and H. Renkidge, R. Keddy, G. Stubbs, F. Burgess, W. Spottiswood and T. Lennon. The side had entered the English Cup for the first time as well as the Cumberland League and the Cumberland Cup, with two teams being entered in the minor Shield competition.

Rivals Red Rose must have put their money troubles behind them and were also enthusiastic about their chances. They had made John Parker the captain, with former skipper David Groggins becoming vice-captain. A number of the old Carlisle Association players were also being linked with a move to Maryport Cottages. The Rose hadn't applied to enter the English Cup but were to compete for the Cumberland County Cup and the Cumberland League with second teams playing in the Cumberland Shield and the Carlisle Charity Shield.

In the September, Shaddongate added a new player when they signed Bellis from Crewe and he made a fantastic debut in a win over Frizington United and they beat Wigton Harriers 4-1 at Willow Holme to continue the good run while a win over Keswick in the English Cup proved another boost. Two months into the campaign and United topped the Cumberland League table with three wins and a loss from their opening fixtures but Red Rose were hot on their heels in second with two wins, a loss and a draw. Shaddongate were, however, sent crashing out of the English Cup when Workington beat them 2-0 at Willow Holme to remain the only Cumberland side left in the competition.

United suffered a further set back in front of a good crowd at Willow Holme when they were beaten 3-1 by Keswick despite Keddy shooting them in front. Marshall and Hodgson (2) struck for the visitors. The

Gate beat The Rose 'B' team 2-1 in the fourth round of the Cumberland Shield and then won 3-0 at Workington's reserve team who had remained in the Cumberland League. United turned up late but soon made the running with A. Simpson shooting the opener following a scrimmage. Stubbs and Wilson added the others after the break. The game was stopped nine minutes from the end for the 'unruly behaviour' of the spectators.

Frizington's McCarten struck twice at Willow Holme but Shaddongate earned a point with goals from Geordie Stubbs and Simpson as the games kept coming in the run up to the busy festive period with a 1-0 scoreline over Scalegill Rovers in the semi-finals of the Cumberland Shield but they lost the return leg. Shaddongate were maintaining pole position in the Cumberland League but were brought crashing back down to earth with a 4-0 drubbing at Red Rose with all the goals coming in the first half but then bounced back with goals from Stubbs and Dalton in a 2-0 success at Moss Bay and followed this up with a home win over Black Diamonds.

Shaddongate were still very much an amateur side but had a couple of registered professionals and an interesting insight into this was displayed when an argument broke out with Workington over the signing of Hughie Campbell. Campbell had been an amateur at United but signed professional and Lancashire League forms when he went to the Reds on a free transfer, with the club offering to find him work if he went to play for them. Campbell was struggling to pay his lodgings in Workington and had an invalid father at home in Carlisle, who he wanted to look after. Workington agreed to pay his travelling expenses and shelled out £3 for railway fares and sundry expenses; it seemed that he wanted to return to playing for

Shaddongate, but Workington wanted the club that signed him to reimburse the money.

Hughie had started out in the 'Gate second team but soon displayed the form that put him into the first team and earned him the subsequent move west. The left back wasn't the quickest but was described as 'nimble and energetic.' Sunderland had also expressed an interest in signing Campbell, 'a genial fellow who was well-liked by his club mates.' Soon he was back at Willow Holme.

Back on the pitch, F.F. Burgess, Ross, captain Graham and G. Simpson all impressed as Shaddongate won 1-0 at Wigton Harriers in the New Year thanks to a penalty but they were held one-all at Black Diamonds in the first round of the Cumberland Cup.

United full-back Jared Johnston was seriously ill from an injury received on Christmas Day but the club rallied around and raised the princely sum £45 for him through exhibition matches by April.

And his-team mates started zeroing in on the Cumberland League title by then with a 4-0 win over Cockermouth at Willow Holme when Keddy, Stubbs, G. Simpson and Barnfather all chalked up strikes. F. Ross was a registered professional at Shaddongate and he got in bother with the County F.A. for appearing for Red Rose and the matter was referred to the Football Association 'recommending they deal severely with the defaulting club and player.'

The matter wasn't enough to put United out of their stride, however and they thought that they had raced home to their first Cumberland Senior Championship with Captain W. Graham all set to lift the silverware. It was being muted as the first time in eight seasons that the trophy had left West Cumberland, and was no mean feat. Graham's popularity was second-to-none in the Border City and he deserved it. He was a centre half-back of sterling service who had been a mainstay over the previous two seasons for Shaddongate. He started out playing for Solway Rovers when at school, along with Jared Johnston, Jack Hutton, and J. Smith, and, along with them, joined Carlisle St. Mary's, and played inside right when they were runners-up for the Carlisle Charity Shield two years in succession. Graham found his proper position, however, when he played half-back for Carlisle Thursday, a team which also included such players as George Young and F. F. Burgess. He also had a season with Carlisle City. Along with Young and Burgess, Graham crossed the Border and played for Annan in their Cup-tie towards the close of the season in question; and the following season (1899-1900) he appeared regularly for Annan, also being chosen vice-captain of Dumfriesshire County team. Graham was a general favourite in the South of Scotland, both with players and spectators. In season 1900/01 he threw in his lot with Shaddongate United, and 'played some splendid games in the Cup ties, his display particularly against Frizington White Star leading to his selection as the Cumberland County centre half against the Liverpool League team, a selection which was but second in popularity to his appointment as captain of the club for the season which is drawing to a close. He has proved himself a capital captain and committee-man.' Graham had only missed one game all season, and that was through illness. The report noted that: 'The 'Gate have now won every competition open them in the county, having risen, one may say, from the lowest rung of the ladder to the top of the Cumberland tree. And all this has come from small beginnings. When the club first won the Carlisle Charity Shield they had no field to practise or play on. Some members of the original team are still 'on the carpet." The celebrations were to prove premature, however, as in an amazing turnaround Keswick were allowed to play a final game after the ordinary end of the season and won it – thus taking the League honours themselves. How embarrassing it must have been for the Carlisle side, not to mention a huge kick in the teeth.

There isn't a great deal of information around on who the officials behind the Shaddongate Club were in 1902, however, the men in the tweed waistcoats and chain watch fobs with stiff Edwardian moustaches that prowled the boardrooms, but Mr. William T. Scott was an early treasurer of the club who was much respected in local soccer circles. Mr. Scott became one of the first Directors when the Gate became Carlisle United and played a prominent role in the move from Willow Holme to Devonshire Park and subsequently on to Brunton Park. He was a member of the Cumberland FA Council from 1912, and treasurer from 1915 to 1938. He was also on the Committee of the Carlisle and District League and president of the Charity Shield – the oldest competition in Cumberland. Mr. Scott was clearly an important mover off the field as Shaddongate looked to continue their rise in Carlisle despite – or maybe because of - the championship farce.

Shaddongate skipper W. Graham

Early official Mr. William T. Scott

5. WHEN THE ROSES COME AGAIN

THE ROAR OF THE WATER tumbling over at Holme Head fills your ears today and it must have been the same for the Red Rose players when they turned out on the pitch at Maryport Cottages, in a field between the residential areas of Denton Holme and Currock, right alongside the weir in the river Caldew.

The Ferguson Brother's red brick textile mill is directly across the water and is another former industrial place that has now been converted into apartments. The Holme Head Works were constructed in 1865 and extended in both 1907 and 1913, so it was a busy and bustling place and the Rose no doubt hoped to capture as fans some of the workers who lived around about in the long terraces off Denton Street. Further down the river in the distance you can see a square tower at the still-going Stead McAlpin works near Cummersdale. The source of the river is up on Skiddaw, the blue smudge of the mountain that towers above Keswick, which also visible among the white clouds on the far horizon of the tree-lined water. The Caldew was the driving force behind the industrialisation of Carlisle, with mills running along it all the way from Shaddongate to Dalston.

"When the Roses come again" was a song that the Red Rose players belted out after their Cumberland Shield semi-final defeat at Cockermouth Crusaders in late 1901 and they were hoping to make more impact in 1902/03 by keeping pace with their Shaddongate rivals. Lennon and Hunton, with a penalty, scored for the Rose in their win at Workington's Ashfield Ground in front of a fair attendance with Elliott pulling one back for Reds in a Cumberland Cup tie. The Carlisle side had almost gone in front in the first minute but Thirsthwaite cleared in the nick of time. O'Hara, Notman, Parker and Skelton all put in decent performances and there was a good gate at the game - considerably more than turned out at Black Diamonds on the same day to see them inflict a 3-0 reverse on Shaddongate, who the newspapers claimed 'weren't the side that they were last season.' After the debacle involving Keswick, it was hardly surprising.

Geordie Stubbs had taken on the mantle of captain at the 'Gate and was described as a popular choice and player. 'The United have had an eventful career, and G. Stubbs has been with them through it all. He was one of the first members, and he is likely play for them for seasons yet to come. He is the holder two three Carlisle Charity Shield medals, one or two Cumberland County Shield Medals, and Cumberland Cup medal and had the season not been extended last year he might very probably have had a Cumberland League medal. Shaddongate won the Carlisle Shield on one occasion when they had neither field, football or any equipment of any kind.'

Stubbs had 'a good turn of speed, uses his head well in both senses reckoned to be the best shooter on the team.' His fellow forwards Keddy and Dickie Routledge were also reputed to be a couple of good players.

United's forward line was further depleted a couple of months later when W. Spottiswoode had two trials with Newton Heath, the Manchester League club who, of course, went on to change their name and become the mighty Manchester United within weeks. Spottiswoode was said to 'have given so much satisfaction at half-back.' His brother Frank played for the Oldham Northern Union club at the same time. 'In Cumberland W. Spottiswoode was more looked upon as an average forward rather than a promising half-back,' reported the Lancashire Evening Post, somewhat snottily.

The Rose were beaten 1-0 by the disputed defending Champions, Keswick, at Greta Grove and were held 2-2 at Cockermouth Crusaders after going behind to a Burns goal in the first minute. Parker shot them level before the break and although Warwick put them in front, Riddell equalised shortly after with a penalty.

A 3-1 win over Workington kept the Rose in third spot while United crashed 5-0 at leaders Black Diamonds and the following week both Carlisle clubs were playing friendlies – the Rose drawing 0-0 at Annan and Shaddongate, playing the match at Boundary Road where the fields of Bishop Harvey Goodwin School are now situated in Currock, beating the Dumfries team Roslyn with former Cummersdale Hornet Robinson grabbing a hat-trick.

W. Graham had retired somewhat prematurely at the end of the season but was back to strengthen the 'Gate with F.F. Burgess and former Carlisle City goalkeeper G. Young also rejoining the side. Burgess was a talented player who had played in every position except between the sticks, and turned out at the half-back for the County when they had played Sheffield Wednesday a few seasons previously; the difference showed with a four-nil win over Cockermouth Crusaders that took them above their City neighbours in the table. When the two sides met in November, they played out a 1-1 draw with the report noting that 'despite the strong rivalry that exists between the two leading Carlisle clubs, the game was contested in a friendly spirit and a large crowd of spectators witnessed an interesting and exhilarating game.'

The City was packed with Association sides at the time as the popularity of the sport continued to grow. The clubs that made it into the second round of the Carlisle Charity Shield competition included Scotby, Willow Holme Mission, N.B. Loco, Shaddongate United's B team, West End B and A, Granville Star, Currock, Red Star A and B, Etterby Rovers, L & NW Rovers, Caxton and Cummersdale Rangers, as well as the top two, so every locality and a number of the railway companies all had teams kicking a heavy leather ball on pitches with tufts of grass sticking up and loose nets hanging from their white frames. The game was booming in the old frontier town.

Red Rose went in front at League leaders Moss Bay Exchange's Westfield ground, but the home side hit back thrice to claim the points. They'd only been beaten once at home in their opening seven games, and that was by bottom side Wigton Harriers. The haphazard nature of the fixture scheduling with friendlies and Cup ties scattered throughout meant that the tables of the time were pretty misleading. The Harriers had only played four Senior League games and Frizington White Star two by the middle of December.

It was noted that there were twenty-four registered professional players in Cumberland in late 1902, with twelve of them being at Workington. 'It should, of course, be understood that the players are not paid regular wages, but simply recompense for broken time in away matches. In home matches the Workington players give their services for free,' a newspaper article helpfully reported. The first professional registered in Cumberland had been a player named Adamson at the old Carlisle Association Club in 1890. But whatever 'boot money' the Red Rose players were getting, the club had to shell out five shillings in a fine imposed by the Association for a game starting late – the first time that financial penalties had been imposed for the offence by the League. Black Diamonds and Moss Bay were also penalised.

The Rose were back in action against Haltwhistle at Maryport Cottages and ran out 3-1 winners, but the main talking point was that Frank Ross, who was registered as a professional at Shaddongate, was back at the club as his transfer went through and he 'gave one of his characteristic displays.' It was alleged that Shaddongate secretary Mr. Wall had 'failed to trace his registration,' but there was a bit of bad blood as Ross had turned out for The Rose *against his own club* the previous season.

United had slipped to the bottom of the League and the 'Gate were in fourth behind Black Diamonds, Moss Bay Exchange and Workington, but had games in hand and these were extended further when the game against the table toppers was cancelled due to a waterlogged pitch for a third time. The Black Diamonds' Cloffocks ground was situated near the Derwent and when the river burst its banks, the grass was left underwater.

They were then beaten 1-0 at Keswick in the Cumberland Cup with Smith the scorer and the Rose linesman was cautioned by the referee twice for giving wrong decisions, but the Carlisle side had built up a two-goal lead in the replayed first leg – Noble netting both. United also advanced into the semis but their tie against Black Diamonds was similarly contentious as ten of the Black Diamonds team walked off in protest after disputing a goal. Willie McClure was then sent off for rough play in front of a record attendance at the Boundary Road ground where the 'Gate were now situated.

Red Rose were drawn to play Workington's Lancashire League side in the last four with the game arranged for a Thursday, but with nine of their players unable to get the time off work they said they would hand the tie to Reds. But this was not without the stinging comments that 'they would have won had they played on a Saturday' and 'hoping you may enjoy the match on Thursday, which you will not see.' It was reputed that the club would be fined two guineas for their pains.

Back in the League, the Red Rose finally played their fixture at Black Diamonds and Hunter scored twice with Warwick getting the other to set up a Championship race between themselves and Frizington White Star. The Rose topped the table having played twelve games, winning seven, drawing three and losing two with 29 goals for and 11 against. Black Diamonds were a point behind but had played a game more while White Star had two games in hand going into the run-in. Shaddongate United had played eleven with three wins, two draws and six losses, wracking up 23 times and conceding 30, so the power balance in the City was definitely shifting. United, however, were hosting Blackpool the following week and were said to be deserving 'every support in their commendable endeavours to bring the Association game to the front in the "Border City".' United were down but not out and clearly had ambitions of moving forward in the sport.

The Rose won one more League fixture before White Star threw in the towel as they couldn't complete their fixtures by the end of the season, thus handing the Carlisle side the title. The celebrations were probably somewhat muted as they waited with bated breath to see if the Association would allow games out of the season, as they had the previous campaign. In all honesty, the season had fizzled to a close however delighted the Rose had been in becoming the first Carlisle side to secure the Cumberland Senior League title. And neighbours Shaddongate weren't resting on their laurels, either. They'd won the Cumberland Cup 3-1 against Workington and had pulled in a huge gate for their game against Blackpool.

'They intend next season to push the game more than ever and, if a central ground can be procured, will probably apply for admission to the Northern Alliance. The Carlisle football public have shown that they will patronise good football,' wrotc 'Cumbriana' in the *Lancashire Evening Post*. Whether they were embittered by the success of their bitter City rivals or not, Shaddongate United were gunning to push for the big time.

	P.	W.	D.	L.	For.	Arst.	Pts.
Carlisle Red Rose	13	8	3	2	32	11	19
Black Diamonds	14	7	2	5	31	32	16
Frizington White Star	10	7	1	2	22	7	15
Moss Bay Exchange	14	7	1	6	33	29	15
Workington	12	6	0	6	30	27	12
Shaddongate United	11	3	2	6	23	30	8
Keswick	12	4	0	8	20	32	8
Wigton Harriers	14	3	1	10	20	44	7

✻ ′ ✻ ✻

44

G. Stubbs

Geordie Stubbs

*This is reputed to be an early Shaddongate United team photo,
but the White shirts might, in fact, be those of Red Rose.*

6. THE BAN

NO DOUBT BOUYED by the success of the City's two senior sides, local football was booming and in August 1903 the Carlisle & District Association Football League was formed – or more formalised, as a League under the same name had been operating – with Mr. T. Hodgson as chairman and Mr. J.A. MacLean as honorary secretary and treasurer. The clubs competing were L and NW Rovers, Scotby, Granville Star, Longtown, Carlisle Red Rose, Cummersdale Rangers, Carlisle West End, Currock and Midland Loco. Invitations had been sent to Shaddongate United, Wigton Harriers, Catholic Y.M.S and Carlisle Red Star asking them to join, while a gentleman from Sheffield had presented a silver cup as a trophy.

Both Shaddongate and Red Rose were reported to be in strong positions for the coming season and the 'Gate had arranged matches with Stockton, the English Amateur Cup holders, and other prominent clubs.

But then an unmitigated disaster struck the Red

Rose club. It was a stupid mistake and vastly over-blown by the Cumberland Football Association, but would prove a blow from which the club never fully recovered and possibly changed the course of football history in Carlisle forever. The entire Red Rose side, and three Shaddongate first team players, were suspended for taking part in a close season five-a-side competition on July 18th, 1903, in connection with the annual Northern Counties Wrestling and Athletic Association. The four-month bans were to run until the 31st of December, which had the virtual effect of killing off the Champions in the Senior League. If they had no players, then they couldn't play, simple as that. The promoters of the tournament had sought permission from the Association but it wasn't given and some of the most prominent players in the City were affected. 'A great deal of feeling has undoubtedly been caused by what is regarded as an unduly heavy punishment,' wrote one newspaper reporter.

Over eighty players had taken part in the games with many travelling from the south of Scotland and up from Penrith and District, but the bulk were local Carlisle lads. Around thirty of them were affected by the ban, as was the official Mr. J.A. MacLean, who was the leading referee in the City as well as a District League official, who had reffed the games.

Jealousy and old ill feeling from the clubs in the West towards those in the East was blamed for the severity of the bans by both Red Rose and the official Mr. McLean, who had played at back for the defunct Carlisle Association's second side before taking up the whistle in 1893.

Mr. Kirkbride, the secretary of Shaddongate United, said that they had lost three first team players and four from the second string and he had approached the Association for permission himself, which wasn't granted, so he'd pulled the club from the tournament but some of the players had turned out for other sides.

"We shall be greatly weakened both for the Cumberland League and the Shield, but happily the Cup contest doesn't start until February," said Mr. Kirkbride.

It was a Workington representative who moved for the suspension of the players and a Frizington representative who seconded, while the movers for the suspension of Mr. MacLean were from Scalegill and Egremont. It led to much bitterness and appeared as if the West clubs were attempting to strangle the further development of Carlisle's football at birth; the junior (in the Scottish sense, or minor) clubs were also greatly affected with Caxton, Red Star and Etterby Rovers all having players banned.

The dispute rumbled on and in October the Cumberland FA met at Workington to discuss the Rose's application for a reduction of the suspension of their players. A number of them were members of the local Volunteers Corps and after playing in the games for money prizes were informed that they could not turn out again until they were registered as professionals or reinstated as amateurs. The application was 'ordered to lie on the table.' Their reserve team were playing in the Cumberland Shield competition and while the first team remained members of the Cumberland League, they hadn't played a game in November as they'd had to postpone all of their fixtures. Funnily enough, it still didn't leave them bottom of the table; Wigton Harriers and Moss Bay Exchange were sitting below them on account of the goals they'd conceded. Workington Black Diamonds were top, followed by Workington, Cockermouth Crusdaders, Shaddongate and Keswick.

With no senior games to watch, some of the Rose supporters could be left kicking their heels some might seek their football fix elsewhere – and that could only benefit Shaddongate. By early December the Cumberland League had decided with, it claimed, the club's consent, that they should take no part in the competition in 1903/04. It was a shattering blow for the defending Champions, although it did have the effect of bolstering their junior sides.

Shaddongate reported Moss Bay Exchange for playing with only eight men in a League match at Carlisle and the offenders were fined 10s as the tit for tat continued. The Cumberland Association then ordered that the date of the Shield Final between Red Rose and Moss Bay, at Workington, be changed from January 9th to December 19th, knowing full well that the Rose would have their suspended players back for the later date. They were prepared to do anything, it seemed, to antagonise the Carlisle clubs – and worse was to follow at the end of the season. But Shaddongate could have no idea of the events that were to unfold and went into the New Year of 1904 in a decent position. The ban's effect hadn't been as damaging to the 'Gate and John Hunton, who had been one of the Rose's suspended stars, turned out for their rivals in a friendly against Glasgow outfit Strathclyde having served his time. Hunton was the 'subject of correspondence between the Cumberland Association and the Scottish Association,' so it can be assumed that he'd impressed enough for the Scots to inquire into signing him up.

Red Rose had originally been formed as a rugby club in 1888 and they'd taken up the Association game a year later. They were beaten by Eden Vale in the Carlisle Charity Shield Final in 1890/91 and in 1892/93 both the club's first and second teams met in the Final of the competition with the first team winning. Early players of note at the Rose included James and John Hunton, T. Hodgson, J. Oswald and T. Bunton. They beat Frizington White Star in the final of the County Shield at Workington on a pitch covered in several inches of snow in January and hoped to return to the Senior League at the end of the season with players of such repute as D. O'Hara, 'a fine full back', D. Groggins, 'a clever and effective centre half', R. Watson, 'a heady and tricky player.' The contemporary crop of promising players included Notman, 'a skilful inside left,' Morley, 'an outside on the same wing,' and Burns, 'a custodian who is usually smart.'

Burns was donning the white shirt of the Red Rose club at just 17 and wasn't one of the players affected by the ban so had played in all the Carlisle and District League games where the Rose had won eight on the bounce, scoring 40 and conceding only three. He was described in a paper at the time as 'a teetotaller and a non-smoker who stands at 5'11' and weighs about 11st.' The Red Rose side that lifted the Shield were A. Burns, W. Oliphant and J. Hamilton; C. Lomas, E. Tinning, R. Groggins; W. Johnston, I. Notman, W. Hutton, E. Hawksworth and J. Skelton.

At the end of January, Shaddongate were second bottom of the Cumberland League table, but they'd only played four games – winning two and losing two – while Black Diamonds and Keswick had played ten and table-toppers Workington seven.

The seeds on dissention where sown in early April when Shaddongate refused to send a team to play a game at Workington, stating that for the return match Workington would be playing in a County Cup tie and would only be sending their reserve team to Carlisle, so the gate would be subsequently effected.

Geordie Stubbs had netted a hat-trick, with two

coming from the penalty spot, as Shaddongate came from two down to beat Keswick 3-2 and set up a barnstorming finish to the Championship run-in as only they were now able to pip the Reds to the title.

The dispute was accentuated when Workington offered to send a side containing seven professionals for the League game, on the same day that they were playing at Keswick in the Cumberland Cup semi-finals, but the 'Gate refused to play anyone but Workington's full strength side. At the time of the dispute, Workington led the League with 8 wins and a draw from their nine games; United had played seven, winning four, drawing one and losing one. They were eight points behind the Ironopolis outfit with five games still to play. Workington's bumper 48 goal haul with nine against dwarfed the Carlisle side's 21 for and 9 against and a win for Workington would in all probability make them uncatchable. But the 'Gate dug their heels in stubbornly, no doubt still resentful at the effect that the ban had imposed on the City.

Red Rose had won all 17 of their Carlisle & District League games with 98 goals scored and just five against to romp to the title in some style ahead of second-placed Currock.

Shaddongate had a stiff penalty imposed by the Cumberland League Committee 'too stiff, they will tell you in Carlisle,' over the matter, which unfortunately isn't recorded but they stuck to their guns. Their argument was that Workington would play their first team at home against them to attract a good attendance, but would only send reserves to Carlisle, which would hit the 'Gate in the pocket. They had strengthened the side for their remaining games, too, by bringing in D. Groggins and D. O'Hara from the Rose and Walton from Carlisle Corinthians, a Thursday League side. Walton also played three-quarter at Carlisle Rugby club, so was a hefty addition. By the 23rd of April Shaddongate were up to second in the table by winning two more games and they trailed Workington by just four points with a game in hand.

The replayed Cumberland Cup semi-final between Workington and Keswick was ordered to be contested in Carlisle and it was noted 'how partial the Carlisle crowd was to Keswick. Recent happenings in the local football world have not made the Reds over-popular in the Border City, somehow or another.' So the Keswick victory was met with some delight, though Workington's Dan Hurst scored the best goal with 'a shot that would have done credit to his League days of some years ago with the Blackburn Rovers.'

But it proved not to be the end of the matter - not by a long shot.

MR. J. A. MACLEAN.

The Official Mr. J.A. MacLean.

A. Burns.

Red Rose –and later Carlisle United- goalkeeper Burns.

R. Gill, who played for Red Rose and later Carlisle Caxton and Cummersdale Hornets.

7. CARLISLE UNITED

CARLISLE UNITED was formed following another bitter football fall out. As we've already seen, the Great Border City was a tough place of textile mills, factories and railway workers at the turn of the last century while 'out West' was the home of pitmen and iron and steel foundry workers. In between you had the rural workers of Lakeland, shepherds, hill farmers, dry stone wallers and farm labourers who enjoyed the traditional sporting pursuits of fell running and Cumberland Wrestling as well as the growing game of Association Football.

The dispute with Workington continued and in late April 1904 Cumberland's senior and most successful side had let their ground to the Cumberland FA for the County Cup Final between Keswick and Cleator Moor United on the same day that they were due to play Shaddongate United in an important Cumberland League match, believing that they could switch the game to Carlisle. But the arrangement again didn't happen, the match was cancelled and the fixtures remained uncompleted. It was all an almighty balls-up and Shaddongate believed that they'd won the Championship – the West teams disagreed and awarded the silverware to the Reds.

It was the second time in three seasons that they felt that they had been robbed of the trophy and it crystallised that divisive 'them and us' mentality that prevails even today. The end of season report issued by the Shaddongate club a couple of weeks later showed they'd taken it in good spirit, in public at least, when they stated: 'We lost possession of the Cumberland Cup and although we claimed the League championship, we were refused it, and must abide by the decision of the West Cumberland members of the Cumberland League.'

In private, however, in was probably the last straw for Shaddongate. A year earlier they'd entertained Newcastle United's reserves and the Magpies must have been impressed with the side as they strongly advised them to change their name to Carlisle United and consider joining the north-east based Northern Alliance.

A report on the match, played in early March 1903, reckoned that the game was fast and exciting throughout with Newcastle's Graham impressing with a brilliant display.

Kerr, G. Stubbs, F. Burgess, Keddy, Campbell and goalkeeper Smith all shone against the Black and Whites, who'd been formed from the Newcastle East End side in 1892. It's a popular misconception that United were formed by an amalgamation of the East End and West End sides – likewise, the legend persists that Carlisle United were formed by an amalgamation of Shaddongate United and their bitter City rivals Carlisle Red Rose.

The club was in a good state financially – the

balance sheet showed an income of £217 for the previous season, with expenditure of £193. Shaddongate had taken £158 5s 11d in gate money. They'd altogether played 30 games in the Cumberland League, winning 11, losing 17 and drawing two, with 63 goals scored and 63 conceded.

Shaddongate, who changed the colour of their strip from Blue and Gold stripes to Blue in 1902, played against Newcastle United again in April 1904 with around three thousand turning out to see the Toon win 4-1 and Fraser hitting a hat-trick for a Newcastle side packed with Scottish professionals. Finley added the other with Spottiswoode netting for the Cumbrians.

This second visit was probably the big influential factor in Shaddongate's decision to apply for the Northern Alliance. At a historic Annual General Meeting of the club on the evening of Tuesday 17th May 1904, Shaddongate United Football Club dropped the localised title and was re-named Carlisle United after a heated discussion, with a few people favouring retaining the clubs' traditional name. A vote on the change was carried by around three to one. It was stated that 'a number of people were at a loss to know who Shaddongate were, and as there was no representative Association club in Carlisle, where the game is enthusiastically supported, it was thought that Shaddongate should be dropped and Carlisle substituted.' It was also reported that the newly-named side were negotiating to get into the Northern Alliance and they were looking to move to a 'more central and commodious ground' with the Association game 'growing rapidly in public favour.'

But at the Northern Alliance AGM in a Wallsend café in June 1904, Carlisle United's bid to join, along with applications from Consett Swifts, Dudley

Wanderers, North Shields Athletic, Shields Town, Newcastle United's third team, Hexham, and Gateshead Town for just three vacancies, was unsuccessful.

Shaddongate had thrashed Hexham 7-2 at Carlisle in September 1903, so they must have at least felt they had a better chance of getting in than the Tynedalers. The Northumbrians had played a more attractive, better passing game however. The voting ballot re-elected Dudley Wanderers and Consett with 11 and 7 votes respectively. There was a tie between North Shields Athletic, Shields Town, and Gateshead, who all received six votes, and in the succeeding vote Gateshead was declared elected.

The Cumberland Association League felt that a disappointed Carlisle United would probably apply for re-admission after failing to get into the Alliance and as it happened they did, falling back in line with the likes of Keswick, Penrith Working Men, Carlisle Red Rose, Workington and Wigton Harriers for 1904/05.

Local rivals Red Rose might have been kicked out of the Senior League but it hadn't stopped the flow of trophies – they were the Cumberland Shield-holders, Carlisle and District League Champions, and for the second successive season, the Carlisle and District Charity Shield Competition winners. They'd won it before on three other occasions – in 1896/97, 1898/9 and 1902/3 to equal the record set by Shaddongate. So the Rose had won every trophy for which they competed in 1903/04 despite the ban, and were reputed to be 'probably the strongest all-round junior team that has held the Charity Shield during the fourteen years of its honoured career.' Having their senior squad playing at the lower level after Christmas obviously helped and they made a successful application to rejoin the Cumberland

Senior League.

In the July of that year at a meeting of the supporters of the late Shaddongate United club, probably the ones that didn't agree with the name change at the AGM, decided to start a new Association club under the old title of Shaddongate United, with 'several prominent Carlisle players promising to throw in their lot with the new organisation,' but it didn't really seem to take off and Carlisle United's first competitive match saw them take on Carlisle Red Rose in a local derby fixture in the Cumberland League on 21st September 1904, which ended in a 1-1 draw, the scorers unfortunately being unrecorded.

The Blues had played a friendly over the Border in Scotland against Maxwelltown Volunteers on the 12th September, so that match has the distinction of being United's first ever game. It also ended in a draw, 3-3 being the score-line.

United were at a bit of a crossroads; they'd looked East along Hadrian's Wall for a league when they may very well have looked North. Carlisle is just nine miles from the Border with Scotland and the side had not only played numerous friendlies in Scotland, but Annan had been known on occasions to help them out with players. While Carlisle were undisputedly an English club, a team crossing the Border to play would soon be set a precedent as Berwick Rangers tired of being given the cold shoulder by the Northumberland F.A., based some sixty miles away in Newcastle-upon-Tyne, and threw in their lot with the Scottish Football Association in 1905 when they joined the Scottish Border League. It was a matter of geography rather than national pride.

Berwick is sometimes confused with being a Scottish town as some people think that the Border is formed by the river Tweed. It does in spells further inland, but the Border itself lies two-and-half miles north of the town near a battlefield site. Flodden Field is the more famous, but Northumberland's most eerie former combat zone is there at Halidon Hill. The place can be haunting and sombre, especially with the steady patter of rain and an unwelcoming, slate-grey sky. Scotland slumped to a crushing defeat at the battle in 1333 as they attempted to take back the besieged town which has changed hands some thirteen times, while Carlisle is famously not included in the Domesday Book as it was part of Scotland before William the Conqueror's son William Rufus took it back in 1092.

At Halidon the Scots' army were picked off by a hail of arrows as they tried to charge across the marshy ground up the hill and were decimated when they finally met the English fighters, breathless and exhausted. English losses were said to be as low as fourteen with the Scottish suffering thousands of dead. Although there are no folk tales of famous phantoms reputed to haunt the spot, but a feeling of dread and unease certainly prevails, especially down on the killing fields towards Bogend farm where hundreds of pig sties now stand. The day started badly for the Scots when their champion, a local Borderer called Turnbull, and his large black dog, were slain in single combat by an English knight from Norfolk called Robert Benhale in a precursor to the main action and it just got worse.

A dark sense of defeat that seems to hang heavy in the atmosphere today and you certainly feel that Turnbull and his faithful dog have never left the scene of their demise with thousands of invisible ghostly fallen comrades with all kinds of awful injuries watching on in their full battle gear through the drizzle. The Scottish leader Sir Archibald Douglas,

William IV Lord of Douglas, Hugh, Earl of Ross, the Earl of Lennox, Alexander de Brus, Earl of Carrick, Kenneth de Moravia, 4th Earl of Sutherland, Alan Stewart of Dreghorn and John Campbell, Earl of Atholl were among the Scottish noblemen that were slaughtered with their men that fateful day. Halidon is a morose spot that encapsulates much of Northumberland's bloody history and if you take the time stand in silence and allow yourself to get immersed in the atmosphere, the ghosts of the Scots' dead will chill you to the bone.

The closest battlefield to Carlisle is probably near Longtown where the famous Kinmont Willie Armstrong is reputed to have fought on at the tender age of fourteen for the winning English side. A Scottish Army of 18,000 were routed by just 3,000 English, including a contingent of 800 Border Reivers such as young Kinmont Willie, who was Scottish himself, at the Battle of Solway Moss in 1542. Only twenty Scots and seven English were reckoned to be killed in the actual battle, but hundreds of Scots drowned in the marshes and the river Esk as they turned tail and fled, with over a thousand notable Scotsmen taken prisoner. My own ancestors were among those Scots borderers who became English for pay and who could blame them? It basically legitimised the raiding that they were doing anyway and ensured that they earned twice from their marauding around the countryside. To understand the Border psyche, you have to know the history. When England and Scotland were constantly at War it was the people in towns like Carlisle and Berwick that bore the brunt, so the Borderland is a place like no other and the people are still there – Carlisle is full of old reiver families like the Armstrongs and Grahams who poured in after the agricultural way of life was urbanised so a good portion of the City is at least partially Anglo-Scottish. As it happened, at the end of the season Carlisle United actually turned their attention South and applied to join the Lancashire Combination League.

The 1904/05 campaign in the Cumberland Senior League unsurprisingly had some controversy from the very start; Robert Barnfather was said to have signed a registration form for United on March 23rd and on September 1st had signed one for Red Rose. The Rose secretary claimed that Barnfather had never signed for United and the secretary of the Cumberland League was to write to the player to find out what was going on.

Red Rose had drawn 2-2 with new side Penrith Working Men at Carlisle early in September to mark their return to the Senior League but in the October, when they beat Workington 4-0 in the second qualifying round of the English Cup with goals from Lennon, Groggins, Watson and an un-named fourth, a bizarre tragedy occurred. A young tailor named William Musgrove, who lived with his parents at William Street in the City, was among the crowd when the ball came off the pitch among them. He kicked the ball back to the players and the next moment he dropped to the ground and died, with a number of the distressed spectators leaving the field soon after.

The Workington side had dumped United out of the competition in the first qualifying round 3-1 in a replay after drawing 2-2 in the City, with the old warhorse Geordie Stubbs United's scorer from a corner.

A number of Carlisle United players were selected to play for Cumberland against Westmorland in the December, with goalkeeper R. Bendle, John Hunton, W. Spottiswoode, G. Morton and W. Morton taking their place in the team alongside F. Ross and D. O'Hara of rivals Red Rose.

Gray, Argyle, Rae and Martland were on target in a 4-1 win over Newcastleton at Carlisle but the Copshaw lads turned the tables in the return match in December as the club who would later become Hearts of Liddesdale won 3-1 with Jackson, Armstrong and Little netting after Rae had given Carlisle an early lead. United also had an 'A' team playing in the Carlisle & District League.

Carlisle secured a new ground in late March when the Duke of Devonshire agreed to lease to six guarantors, on behalf of the club, the field off Lismore Place which was at one time occupied by the Carlisle Rugby Club. The lease was for fourteen years and the club 'proposed to properly barricade the field, erect grandstands and lay the enclosure out as a football and athletic ground.'

United took the six team Cumberland Senior League at a canter. They won eight of their ten games, drew one and lost one with 26 goals for and 11 against. Red Rose finished second with four wins, three losses and three draws, scoring fifteen and conceding nine, so the stage was all set for a Cumberland Senior Cup Final showdown between the two old rivals. A bumper crowd provided record gate receipts of £106 8s and United claimed the Double with a 2-0 win. There was a deafening roar when Parker shot into the Rose net in the second half and the trophy was secured a couple of minutes from the end when former Preston North End star Tom Smith added number two.

The mighty Glasgow Rangers also came down to Carlisle that month and won 2-1. Steel shot into an open goal to put the 'Gers one-up after twenty minutes and Wilson added a second five minutes later.

Stubbs headed in from a corner in the second half and United came close to equalising on a couple of occasions. They had clearly become the preeminent side in the City and the club officials, with a bit of swagger and looking like they'd just stepped off the set of *Peaky Blinders* in their three-piece tweed suits and flat caps, were looking to push United on beyond the mountains and Lakes of Cumberland.

H. CAMPBELL

Hughie Campbell, the early Shaddongate star.

8. THE LANCASHIRE COMBINATION

I N MAY 1905 Carlisle United made an ambitious application to join the Second Division of the Lancashire League along with Little Hulton United, Burnley Reserves, Glossop, Haslington, Clitheroe Central, Failsworth and Lancaster. Both United and Lancaster offered to pay twelve railway fares and provide teas for visiting players for two years and five clubs were elected to membership – Lancaster with 27 votes, Bolton St. Luke's (re-elected with 26 votes), Newton-Le-Willows (re-elected with 20 votes), Burnley Reserves with 17 votes and the 16 that Carlisle received being just enough to see them in.

Lancashire had long been a force in Association football with the clubs from the mill towns scattered around the Pennine moors prominent in the early development of the Football League with Accrington, Blackburn Rovers, Bolton Wanderers, Burnley and Preston North End all being among the original twelve member clubs in 1888. You could probably throw Merseysiders Everton in amongst them too.

Former Celtic and Lincoln City player J. Henderson

was among the first signings that United made that summer as they prepared for the step up in standard. All of the team had been offered professional terms during the previous season, which had seen an increase of £50 in the clubs running expenses, and they had retained practically all of the side including Tom Smith and former Rose star David Groggins while Newcastle United were to travel West to help out in 'securing and equipping the new ground,' at Lismore Place, which was dubbed Devonshire Park after the man who had leased them the field - Lord Devonshire. Newcastle won 4-0 with goals from Harding (2), Donnachie and Dodds in front of a large crowd. The Toon were originally to send a reserve side, but the directors of the club 'who have always shown an interest in the progress of Association football at Carlisle, resolved to put the greater portion of the First League players into the team.' It was a big deal really as Newcastle had the best team in the country at the time which they proved when they won their first Football League Championship that season.

United were drawn against their old rivals Red Rose in the opening tie of the English Cup competition and were elected members of the Football Association along with Clapton Orient in August. The Red Rose were still competing in the Cumberland Senior League against United's reserves, Wigton Harriers, Penrith (who had signed Penrith cricket club professional Beadsworth, a former Preston North End and Manchester United player), Keswick, Frizington White Star, Moresby Parks and Cockermouth Crusaders. The Rose were feeling the pressure; they'd been so concerned about their prospects that they sent in their resignation from the League but had recanted and withdrew it.

Things were moving along quickly at the Blues,

however, and United kicked-off the season with a 3-2 defeat at their 'splendid new ground in Devonshire Park' by St. Helens Town. United had bossed the early stages but went behind when they were hit on the break and Smith netted 'a low, rolling shot.' Hodgson added a second before the break. Tom Smith pulled one back almost immediately after the restart and 'amid tumultuous cheering,' Hunton just missed a second. Smith banged the leveller into the net which 'put the spectators into a fever of excitement,' but St. Helen's won it when their Smith headed cleverly in from a corner. Although they'd been beaten, Carlisle had got a taste for what the new adventure was going to be like and they'd enjoyed it, the supporters said to be 'exceedingly well pleased with the display.' The club had taken £35 on the gate though the weather wasn't great and they were hoping for a bigger turn-out for the visit of Blackpool in the next game. United made one change with Fisher replacing Hetherington, but in United went down 5-1 in front of a bumper crowd. Tom Smith was again the scorer.

United secured a 3-0 success at Burnley Reserves with Henderson, Morton and Hunton, with a penalty, the scorers. The side lined up as follows: Bendle; Spottiswood and Hamilton; Foster, Groggins and Routledge; Hunton, Houston, Smith, Henderson and Morton. The Blues then moved to strengthen their ranks by signing on professional forms prolific Castletown striker Archie Musgrave, who hailed from the town but had thrown in his lot with Castletown after being one of the players suspended in the notorious ban two years previously.

A crowd of 3,000 turned out to see United beat Red Rose 3-0 in the eagerly anticipated English Cup First Qualifying Round at Devonshire Park. Tom Smith struck twice after a goalless first half and Hunton got the other. The first home victory in the Lancashire Combination followed a week later when United beat Newton-Le-Willows in a seven-goal thriller,

United were having no problems finding the back of the net and their forward line was reputed to be 'the best to be seen in the Second Division of the Combination.' Scotsman J. Henderson was impressing at inside-left and had 'displayed some of the prettiest and most effective football ever seen in Carlisle.' Henderson came from Maxwelltown and his 'trickiness and dodging abilities' had been 'the admiration and amusement of the United supporters.' The former Celtic man was clearly an early fan favourite and was reputed to be very unselfish, 'never parting with the ball for the mere sake of getting rid of it.' Henderson had talked his old team-mate Colvin to sign up and United also added a player called Lorimer and Kerr, formerly of Longtown, was also an addition.

The new faces were included against Manchester City reserves at Carlisle and Colvin and Henderson combined to create an opening for Smith, but City keeper Yinde parried the resultant shot wide for a corner. United were well on top in the first half but fell behind when Vaughan netted in a melee. Adam struck City's second straight after the turnaround and then added a dubious third, which was 'unmistakably demonstrated' by the large crowd.

While United were away playing Barrow in the Second Qualifying Round of the Cup, where they went out, the Red Rose organised a friendly against Lancaster but the newspapers bemoaned the fact that they hadn't tried to play it at United's empty Devonshire Park ground with their own, the 'Gate's old pitch up at Boundary Road, being 'inconvenient.'

The Cup defeat didn't dishearten Carlisle and they

bounced back to hit Haslingden for six in front of another 3,000 turn out in the Combination. Henderson shot against the woodwork but McKillop followed up to head the rebound into the net for the opener and a second-half goal blitz from Smith (2), Groggins (2) and Henderson left the visitors 'quite outclassed.' United's supporters were left dumbfounded however, as they then went down 8-1 at Clitheroe and then went down to a disputed last minute winner scored by Burnley after dominating the game.

United's 'A' team met the Rose in the Cumberland League at Milhome Bank but the side was virtually the same as the one that had won the Double the previous season with all the new faces in the first team. The Rose scored a creditable victory as goals from Barnfather, Johnstone and Gardner put the Rose on top with Matthews pulling one back after the break. It would prove the final meeting between the two Carlisle clubs.

In late December, Red Rose lined up: A. Burns, E. Tinning and D. O'Hara; Lomas, D. Groggins and Skelton; Barnfather, Hutton, Johnstone, Gardner and Notman for a club match at Kendal Swifts. The side found themselves in hot water with the Cumberland League Executive again in January 1906 when they were fined a guinea and docked four points, when they had virtually won the League Championship, for fielding an illegible player. The *Lancashire Evening Post* reported that: 'The Rose supporters contend that this penalty, for an offence which was unwittingly committed, is not only out of all proportion, but inclines them to feel through previous experiences that the Cumberland League is "no place for them."' Some of the committee thought they should withdraw from the League immediately, while others felt it would be suicidal; the Rose chairman, Mr. William

Whittle, denied that any meeting of the committee had taken place, however, and wrote that the idea of withdrawing had never even been thought about, it being 'very unsportsmanlike.'

The Rose were putting the heading "Patronise Local Talent" on the posters advertising their games around Carlisle in somewhat of a dig at United and a desperate attempt to lure some of their crowd away. They were said to be handicapped primarily on account of their ground and secondly by the quality of their matches – though they 'were undoubtedly a smart team.'

The harsh four-point deduction saw them trailing in second spot to Frizington White Star in the Cumberland League but they completed their programme with a 4-0 drubbing of Moresby Parks and then drew 1-1 when they met White Star in the Cumberland Cup Final at Workington. The Rose won the replay 2-1 to lift the silverware, but it the game was said to be 'one of the poorest ever played on Workington's ground.' Rose captain O'Hara admitted it had been a poor game, 'but as the Star had the League Cup, he did not think they would envy the Rose the county trophy.' Both sides had applied for financial assistance and were granted £5 each by the Cumberland FA after the game. The Rose were wilting while United continued their rise and in the August of 1906 the old club simply 'dropped from existence'. A few sad lines in the *Athletic News* noted that 'with the growth in support of the matches of its local rivals the United club, the gates of the Red Rose club have dwindled away to almost vanishing point.' The divided loyalties in the City were finally over; Carlisle would now be joined behind just one side – United.

The Blues had been having some problems with some with their players over a few weeks and the

Carlisle committee were 'determined to exercise a firm hand with regard to players if in any way they did not act in a manner conducive to the success of the club. Rumours, with all too much truth in them, have been flying about, and these have resolved the committee to take firm action.' What the players had been up to is anyone's guess as the newspapers don't go into further detail – but it may have involved drink as the report continued: 'in competition football nothing less than the very best of players' form is sufficient, and anything players may do to make themselves unfit for the demonstration of that form must be checked at all hazards. A wink is as good as a nod to a blind horse, but it is to be hoped certain players may take the hint.'

Tom Smith had been unavailable after being struck down with a very serious illness so Matthews was given another chance at outside right with Hunton alongside him. Groggins found himself dropped to be replaced by Forster and Lorrimer replaced Spottiswood, nicknamed, of course, 'Spotty,' so the team still contained a big element of local lads.

Right half back Forster, a painter by trade, was reckoned to command the respect of the Devonshire Park crowd and had 'held his own in the best company he has yet met in the Combination matches. His perseverance and energy, supplemented by a systematic study of the game, make him almost indispensible.' He was a staunch teetotaller, and knew how to take care of himself 'both for his own benefit and for the good of the club.'

Forster had started out in a boy's team called Princess Villa and later joined C.Y.M.S. and was spotted by the Carlisle committee while playing in a representative game for the Carlisle and District against the Carlisle Thursday League.

Forster was described as 'having a fine shot and was clever and fearless tackier. Besides football, be also follows other branches of athletics. He is clever with the boxing gloves, and his favourite exorcise is on the parallel and horizontal bars, which he believes to be excellent for keeping young men in a fit condition for the requirements the football field.' Those complaints were almost certainly drink-related.

The Blues had tried three new players in a club game against Grimsby Town with Wills, McLean and Findlay, signed from Newcastle United, coming into the side but were frustrated when they were forbidden to play against Chorley in the Combination on the same day as the Cumberland Cup Final by the Cumberland Association who were 'over zealous in looking after their own interests.' The same couldn't really be said of the Blues, who had organised a benefit match to assist the struggling Red Rose club in April. But relations with the local FA had been deteriorating since February when Mr. Wall, of the English Association, had read a letter from Mr. McCumisky of the club complaining about them being ordered to keep that date open. The action of Carlisle United 'was strongly condemned, and looked upon as an insult to the (local) Association.' There was also bitter talk of the Cumberland Association opposing their re-election to the Lancashire Combination if they failed to adhere to the instruction.

When United met Workington at Devonshire Park in one of the final games of the season it set a record take on the gate of £208 3s 4d, smashing the previous big take of £108 in the Cup tie against the Rose the previous season. A 1-1 draw effectively killed Workington's chances of promotion to the First Division, while Carlisle had enjoyed a relatively successful first season at the higher level and at a lively AGM, presided by Mr. C.K. Coulthard, showed a balance sheet of £2,566 13s 4 ½ d in income and an expenditure of £2,538. The club passed a resolution that it be turned into a private limited liability company with a capital of £2,000 in £1 shares while the grandstand was to be enlarged and the ground accommodation improved and the club were considering entering their second string in the Northern Counties League. The Officers elected that evening were Mr. W.C.G Hetherington as president, Mr. Houston as secretary, Mr. George McCumisky the financial secretary with Mr. Tom Graham the treasurer and Mr. Scott the assistant treasurer.

As it happens, the Northern Counties changed name and they ended up becoming founder members of a League of professional teams suggested by Newcastle United – The North Eastern League – along with reserve sides from Sunderland, Middlesbrough, Newcastle United, Leeds City and Bradford City, and the first teams of West Stanley, Sunderland Royal Rovers, Hebburn Argyle and Workington. United must have felt that the class of football in that League was going to be better and it was in fact the first team that entered the North-Eastern, with the reserves continuing in the Lancashire Combination.

The club were becoming more ambitious and signed George Thompson, a forward, from Crystal Palace as well as picking the bones of the defunct Red Rose club and signing their keeper Andrew Burns. They also picked up J. Lyons, a centre forward from Swindon Town, George Pickering from Dudley, J. Bradbury from Millwall Athletic, J. Johnson from Grimsby Town and Anthony Carter from Bradford City as the days of strictly local players came to an end.

Carlisle United team photo in 1904/05. Back Row: Forster, Wishart, Scott, Hamilton, Birch. Front Row: Hunton, Smith, Kirkby, Henderson, Connon, Groggins.

Carlisle United in 1905/06. Back Row L-R. Kirkbride (Secretary), McCumisky (Chairman), Lorimer, Scott, Hamilton, Dalton (Trainer). Middle: Hunton, Smith, McKillop, Henderson, Colvin. Front: Burge, Groggins, Forster. The team seem to be wearing the old Shaddongate shirts of gold and navy blue stripes.

J. Henderson.

Carlisle United's Scottish ace J. Henderson and below, W. Forster.

W. Forster.

9. THE NORTH EASTERN

T HE EARLY POPULARITY of Rugby in Carlisle and Cumberland in general, as well as the isolated rural upland location, had somewhat hindered the early development of the Association game in the county and United were playing catch up with the big established clubs in Lancashire and the North-East.

They were, however, handily positioned for the rail network that carried players to and from games in those days. It must have been a great day out for the teams in the carriages as they chugged through the countryside in a billow of coal smoke, perhaps playing cards at the tables, player's jackets draped over the arms of the seats and maybe the odd Woodbine being sparked up.

United's rise in popularity had hit the local amateur game and Carlisle & District League secretary Mr. T. Hodgson said that the previous season had been disappointing 'owing to the greater attraction given to the public by the better class football introduced by the seniors, and the enterprise of Carlisle United.' The local League was continuing to expand, though, and had received applications from North Eastern Railway, Eskdale Juniors (Longtown), East End, Carlisle Teachers, Cummersdale United and Border Depot.

United split their side and lined up Scott; Collins and Gunzeon; Blyth (capt), Foster and Burge; Thompson, Maher, Lyons, Cowie and Johnson for the opening Lancashire League appointment at Port Sunlight, which they won 3-1, and on the same day another United team were taking on a Workington team in the Cumberland Senior League with the side being: - Carlisle United: Burns, Clarke and Carter (capt); Smith, Raisbeck and Fisher; Bradbury, Sanderson, Pickering, Notman and Gardner – a side containing some of the old Red Rose team as well as a few of the big-name signings who were probably being given a leg-stretching run-out.

United drew 1-1 at Hebburn Argyle in their first game in the North Eastern League. Keeper Burns was winded in a goalmouth tussle and had to leave the field, but soon returned. He was beaten by Williams on the half hour for the opener but Gardner equalised in the second half. Carlisle then 'enhanced their good reputation in the North Eastern League' when they beat Sunderland 'A' 4-2 in front of 5,000 fans with Maher netting twice – the first after just three minutes – Lyon and Pickering adding the others after the break.

It was reckoned to be 'some time before Carlisle United would forget their visit to Skelmersdale' in the Lancashire League in October 1906. The Skelmersdale players were described as 'a tough and determined lot on their own ground at any time, without the crowd of spectators crying for the blood of a visiting player.' The crowd started lobbing pieces of the cinder track at the Carlisle side and it got too much for Johnston after a bit hit him on the head so he went over and 'took the prompt and English redress of stepping to the barriers and 'explaining the position' to the transgressor.' Not quite an Eric Cantona moment, but not far off.

Sanderson netted in a 1-1 draw at Sunderland Royal Rovers but Carlisle suffered their first defeat of the season in the Combination at Stockport, with Pickering the pick of the side. With teams playing in three Leagues – the Lancashire Combination, the North Eastern League and the Cumberland Senior League, as well as all the Cup competitions, United's team selectors must have had quite a headache. United players J. Hunton and J. Notman appeared for Cumberland in the inter-League game against Westmorland in late October and the side (which one, I'm not entirely sure!) advanced in the English Cup with a 3-0 win over Penrith in front of several thousand with Lyon, Sanderson and Hunter on the scoresheet but the club had to postpone a North Eastern engagement against Bradford City when they met Barrow in the next round where they won 2-1 in front of 4,000. Maher and Smith scored. The Blues went out 4-0 in the fourth qualifying round in front of another bumper crowd against Southport Central, but it had been a good run.

Carlisle's team that travelled to Oswaldtwistle Rovers in the Combination contained the players Scott; Collins and Gungeon; Thomson, Forster and Gardiner; Smith, Mayer, Lyon, Sanderson and Johnson so it could be assumed United were mixing their top players between the two teams in the Leagues outside the County; United were in ninth spot in the twenty-team Combination but had beaten the highly-fancied Leeds City's reserves 2-0 in Carlisle with the goals coming from Cowie and Winter as they sat behind the big reserve teams of Newcastle United and Middlesbrough in the North Eastern with games in hand on all the clubs around them, winning three and drawing two of their first five matches. The situation must have been putting pressure on the players and a few cracks possibly started to show when left back A. Gardiner was suspended for 14 days by the Cumberland FA for using bad language to the referee in the game at Oswaldtwistle.

Towards the festive period a massive 12,000 turned out to see Carlisle beat Workington 4-2 in the Combination with 'intense excitement' in the ground. Lyons got the first following a good run by Thompson and Maher cleverly netted the second. Thompson crossed for Gardiner to put away the third in a magic thirteen-minute spell. Robertson and Pearson reduced the arrears after the break and 'excitement was at fever pitch' until Sanderson put away a fine centre by Thompson to finish the scoring off. Around the same time United beat Middlesbrough reserves 3-1 on a snow-covered Devonshire Park with Hunton crossing for Cowie to put away the opener within two minutes of the kick-off. Notman added a second before the break and the 'Boro keeper was stooping to roll a snow-covered back out of the back of his net a third time when defender Barker sliced past him in attempting to clear. Tucker put away a penalty at the other end after Clark had handled.

It was doubtful whether Carlisle would enter the Cumberland Cup with such a heavy fixture list and they put in a request to the Cumberland FA that the trophy be decided on a knock-out basis rather than the 'League home and home' system, but the Association 'could not see their way to adopt this course and Carlisle's name was submitted to the draw.'

Further brushes with officialdom followed as United reported the referee for 'incompetency' after a game against Bradford City reserves that saw one player break his collarbone and another badly kicked with Chairman Mr. C.K. Coulthard explaining how in his opinion the referee had allowed the game to degenerate. While the North Eastern League Management Committee dismissed the charge, they did agree that the whistle-blower had 'not been physically fit to undertake the match.' The furious Carlisle crowd had gathered around him at the end of the game and he had to be protected by the United officials and the police.

The United side that went down 3-0 at Leeds City's Elland Road ground in February lined up: Kifford; Clarke and Blythe; Smith, Forster, Raisbeck; Bradbury, Pickering, Winter, Sanderson, Johnson while in the same month residents of 'the fashionable East end of Carlisle were becoming agitated over the scheme of the Carlisle United Football Club to lay out a new ground on Warwick Road.' The first seeds of the modern club were being sown, but they were being met with protest. The residents were complaining that if the development was allowed it would devalue their properties and 'cause an intolerable nuisance owing to the crowds that attend these football matches, whose conduct and language is most undesirable in a respectable and quiet neighbourhood.' The people on Warwick Road petitioned the Carlisle Health Committee and it was referred to the General Purposes Committee. The future of the club was in the balance.

On the pitch, however, United's Combination side were being described as 'virtually invincible' at nearby Devonshire Park and they demonstrated this with a 6-0 drubbing of Haslingden and a 7-1 thrashing of Newton-Le-Willows to put them two points clear at the top of the table, but it was the North Eastern side that was being described as United's 'League' team at the time in contradiction to a number of existing records.

The financial implications of fielding teams on three fronts were also starting to tell and United announced a debt balance of £133 with the directors investing around £1,100 up to that point in the season. The crowds had been on the up, but United were concerned that 'a lot of people were getting into the ground without paying, by using the tickets of other members.'

A 9-0 drubbing of Frizington in the Cumberland League was notable not just for the scoreline, but the fact that the visitors turned up an hour late and had no shirts with them, so had to borrow 'Carlisle United's new coloured shirts, black and white.' Surely not, I hear you groan. But it's there, in, dare I say, black and white in the Lancashire Evening Post. The date, however, may be relevant – April 1st 1907. Whatever the prank, United's North Eastern League team took the Cumberland League silverware by winning seven of their ten games, drawing one and losing two with 34 goals for and 12 against. Second-placed Penrith played nine, their match against Frizington being unplayed, winning six, losing two and drawing one with 21 goals for and 15 against.

United lifted the Lancashire Combination Second Division Championship trophy on the same day with a 3-1 win over St. Helens. The Blues topped the table with a record of 38 games played, 23 wins, 10 draws and just 5 losses, 115 goals being netted and 46 conceded. Earlston finished four points behind in second. The Blues also picked up medals in the Cumberland Cup Final, albeit runners-up ones, as they were beaten by 2-1 by Workington in front of 10,000 at the Carlisle Rugby Club ground.

Fisher scored a brilliant long range goal as United beat Sunderland Royal Rovers 1-0 in the North Eastern League, which was won by Newcastle United reserves. United's promising start faded away and they finished eighth with 5 wins, 9 losses and 4 draws from their 18 games with 23 for and 36 against. Bradford City and Hebburn Argyle were the two clubs below them.

The preparations for the following season in the top flight of the Lancashire Combination soon got underway but Herbert Lyons left the club to join Swindon Town and keeper Andrew Burns joined Penrith while Carlisle were still to pay the railway fares of First Division clubs who asked for it – Preston North End, Everton and Manchester United generously stating that they would not ask for expenses for teas or railway fares.

Stockport player White was signed up but a contract wrangle ensued with Clyde over the signing a player called Tom McAteer who had signed for the Scottish club but hadn't been registered within fourteen days, so he joined the Cumbrians. United's raids into Scotland continued with the signing of James Bauchop from Hearts and the club reported a loss at the meeting of the directors with £1,810 being paid in wages and a total expenditure of £2,744 with receipts of £2,592, but the meeting was 'of the most encouraging character.' Mr. Scott and Mr. Kirkpatrick were re-elected directors and Mr. Postlethwaite replaced Mr. J.C. Barling.

United were drawn to play against a new rival side – Carlisle City – in the first preliminary round of the English Cup. City had applied to join the North-Eastern League but were unsuccessful and received just three votes. Shildon, Bradford and neighbours

Penrith were admitted so City went into the Cumberland League along with Dalston Red Rose and Haverigg St. Luke's. The Cumberland Association would only allow United and Workington to compete in outside competitions on the condition that they entered both the Cumberland Cup and the Cumberland Senior League, and 'the relations existing between the leading Cumberland clubs and the Cumberland FA were intensified' as United had expressed an interest in withdrawing from the Senior League. United, of course, felt that they were receiving unfair treatment and the costs associated with running 'two first rate professional teams in the Lancashire Combination First Division and the North Eastern League' would leave them with heavy expenditure. Secretary Mr. McCumisky noted that if the friction with the Cumberland FA continued then they would 'appeal to the English Football Association to appoint a commission to inquire into the whole circumstances.'

On the opening day in the Lancashire Combination top flight McAteer put in Adair to fire in the opener at Barrow and although United keeper Fletcher saved a Rimmer penalty, they were held to a point when Gibson levelled. United were 1-0 winners at Manchester City and Bobby Tait hit the winner 'with a magnificent single-handed effort' at Manchester United during a fantastic start in the step up in quality. Workington, who had finished fourth, were also promoted.

The start in the North Eastern wasn't as great, but things were turned around when Leeds City travelled for a mid-week meeting at Devonshire Park and were soundly thrashed 5-1 with goals coming from Smith (2), Alf Robinson, Tait and a McAteer penalty. The team lined up: Fletcher; Collins and McKenzie;

Spottiswood, McAteer and Black; White, Smith, Tait, Robinson and Campbell. There were, however, some troubles within the camp and the club suspended four players – A. Clark, T. Drain, T. Sanderson and H. Powell – for reasons that weren't stated in the press.

The Carlisle City side that were beaten 1-0 at United in the English Cup lined up: W. Douglas; H. Scott and E. Fisher; G. Graham, R. Groggins and M. Beattie; G. Sim, A. Musgrave, E. Henderson, C. Hulme and J. Hunton – a team which obviously contains a few old United and Red Rose local stars. United appointed their first secretary/manager around this time with Mr. James Burton Stansfield, formerly connected with Rossendale United, taking on the important role and soon after the Council of the English FA ruled that United did not have to play in the Cumberland Senior League, it not 'being a competition promoted and managed by the County Association.' That wasn't the end of the matter however, and in December the County FA was threatening to suspend the club for not submitting a properly audited balance sheet 'from their practice matches and charity matches during the close season.' It smacked of pettiness but United weren't concerned as they swiftly provided the paperwork.

Newcastle United's reserves were 2-0 winners at Devonshire Park as United sat in third bottom after six games in the North Eastern, winning two and losing four, while new boys Penrith were rock bottom with three losses and two draws. A 3-2 win at Workington helped, with Robinson hitting a double and Campbell the other.

Although United had secured the new ground behind Brunton Place despite the local protests, they felt that it wouldn't be ready in time for the next season and the Duke of Devonshire agreed a slight extension on the club's lease on their ground.

The highlight of the season was to prove in the English Cup where United beat Lancaster 4-1 with Robinson netting twice, Tait and White getting the others, then thumped Windermere 9-1 in the next qualifying round with Maher hitting four, Robinson three and Tait and McAteer also on target as they started to put a run together. The English Cup was considered the premier competition in the country at the time, even surpassing the Football League in terms of prestige and the amazing run continued with a seven-goal mauling of Darlington where Bauchope grabbed a hat-trick and Maher and Robinson two apiece. The excitement kept mounting as United disposed easily of Southend 4-0 and were drawn at home to Brentford in the first round proper. Brentford offered Carlisle all of the gate money minus £50 if they re-arranged the game down South, saying that the 'take' from their previous two ties had been £700. It must have been tempting for the United board, but they politely declined the cash. It was a smart move – the United team of Fletcher; Collins and Carter; Blyth, McAteer and Black; Powell, Maher, Tait, Robinson and Bauchope lined up in dull weather in front of 6,000 packed into Devonshire Park and Powell scored twice as United held their highly-fancied visitors to a 2-2 draw.

The replay was held down at Brentford and 10,000 turned out to see it. The Southerners went ahead on the greasy surface when Tomlinson netted from a corner after just five minutes. But in the second half Robinson headed in the leveller from a free kick to take the game to extra time. Ten minutes into the first period United were awarded a penalty and McAteer kept his cool to fire home then Robinson added a killer third. They'd not only earned a couple of bumper pay days, but United had arrived on the national stage and it all seemed a long way away from Shaddongate. United were drawn away to Grimsby Town in the second round and Lady Luck wasn't on their side as McAteer missed a penalty in the first ten minutes and a crowd of 8,000 watched on as Town ran out 6-2 winners in the end. The profits from the Cup run didn't have a big impact on the club's finances and while the Lancashire Combination team was paying its way, the North Eastern League side had lost around £400. With the £1,000 cost of 'the compulsory removal to the new ground at Brunton Park' staring them in the face, Carlisle were considering running a team of local lads in the North Eastern the following season while 'keeping up the high standard of the professional for the Lancashire Combination matches.'

That quality was certainly on display as United won 4-3 at Liverpool's Anfield ground thanks to strikes from Sanderson, Blythe, Tait and Bauchop and victories over the likes of Atherton, St. Helens and Bury Reserves saw United in third spot behind leaders Everton and Workington in early April with 17 wins, six defeats and seven draws from the 30 games they had by then played. United completed the double over Manchester United reserves – whose first team won the Football League that season - when the ball crashed back off the upright and Tait was on hand to fire home the only goal of the game which was met with loud cheers.

Despite the ball sticking in the mud on a heavy pitch that resembled a quagmire, Carlisle beat Barrow 4-0 in the final game of the Lancashire Combination season with Tait netting a hat-trick, and earning himself a move North to Motherwell, while Sanderson scored the other as United finished runners-up to Everton reserves.

The club's annual report in June showed a heavy loss of £238 14s, which the directors blamed squarely on the 'extremely unsatisfactory performances in the North Eastern League and the consequent lack of interest and greatly diminished attendances.' Work at Brunton Park was proceeding satisfactorily with the preparation of the playing pitch carrying on and while the club had taken £3,000 in gate money during the season, outgoings included over two grand in player's wages, £262 10s in travelling expenses, £68 in visitor's travelling expenses, £146 in hotel expenses and £85 for referees and linesmen. Cash –or the lack of it - was starting to become a problem.

United's Scottish Centre forward Bobby Tait

Brown, of Brentford, gets the ball from a throw in.

Fletcher, the Carlisle goalkeeper, rushes out and clears.

A couple of action shots from Carlisle's English Cup tie against Brentford. Below: Early manager Mr. J.B. Stansfield.

The Carlisle players E. Fisher and David Maher.

D. MAHER, Carlisle United.

10. MONEY TROUBLES

U NITED'S PREPERATIONS for the 1908/09 season on the field saw them sign up a number of the previous season's team, as well as making a few additions. In July, the squad contained goalkeepers J. McIntyre and George Anthony (from Haltwhistle), backs A. Carter and J. McKenzie, Fred Rose (Blackpool), Hugh Campbell (Workington) and George Graham (Dalston), half backs. W. Blyth, J. Wishart, W. Forster and E. Fisher and Thomas R. Gardiner (Penrith) and the forward line was D. Maher, S. Kirkman, Robinson, T. Sanderson, W. Bauchop. Robert Baxter and Joseph Pattinson were added from Carlisle Butchers while negotiations were on-going with a good class goalkeeper and a couple of forwards throughout the summer months, with former Stockport and Fulham player Poss, Wykes, from Stourbridge, Flannery and Tatler from Newcastle Staffs. and Potter of Penrith coming in before the big kick-off, as well as a 'large number of local footballers.'

There was a heated meeting at the Cumberland FA at Workington when six men – reputed to be representatives of new clubs – were in fact directors of Carlisle United and although they tried to force their way into the room, the door was held amid 'scenes of much excitement.' United's manager and secretary Mr. Stansfield threatened to report the matter to the English F.A. after the meeting voted 42 to 4 against letting the United contingent in to cast their votes.

The County FA chairman blamed the Carlisle crew for the incident and said 'it seemed to him that they wanted to rule Cumberland' and were 'attempting to worry him out of his intension to hold the balance between the clubs, but he was thick-skinned enough to stick to his post until he was "chucked."' The Cumberland League was almost wound up in September with both United and Workington withdrawing to concentrate on their Lancashire Combination and North-Eastern League commitments and it was noted in the Yorkshire Evening Post that 'the population of Cumberland is concentred in one or two centres and, except, perhaps, in Rugby Union Football, where there is absolute amateurism and little expense, it is impossible for decent football clubs to exist.' The reporter also felt that, outside the big two, there was 'practically no interest in any other Association football.'

The Blues' North Eastern League side lined up Bell; McKenzie and Nixon; Smith, Hulme and Black; Thompson, Perks, Baxter, Notman and Potter for their trip to St. James' Park to play Newcastle United 'A' while a side containing McIntyre; Rose and Carter; Blyth, Wishart and Forster; Kirkman, Maher, Poss,

Sanderson and Bauchop faced Manchester United reserves at Devonshire Park, so a clear distinction was no being drawn between the first and reserve teams with the main focus now being on the Combination team.

Penrith found the travel over to Tyneside, Wearside and Yorkshire too much and had dropped out of the North Eastern after just one season. Finishing bottom of the table hadn't helped either, mind, and when United's reserves met Workington's in their first home fixture in the league it was described as 'a poor display, with glimpses of good play few and far between.' United were noted for adopting the 'short passing game' that had been popularised in Scotland and brought over the Border to Newcastle United by the large number of Scots players in their ranks in those Edwardian times, while the Reds played a more direct 'dashing' style to win 2-1.

The black and white shirts of Newcastle were seen in Carlisle towards the end of September when they sent their first team over to play a game to raise funds for an extension to the Cumberland Infirmary and the Blues surprised them with a 4-3 win in front of a large attendance. Sanderson and Baxter both struck twice before Newcastle got into gear and Allan hit a hat-trick in reply, each goal being set up by outside right Jackie Rutherford, who finished second top scorer at the club after netting 15 times in the First Division of the Football League that season. The game was a big enough deal for a report to appear in the *London Daily News*.

Carlisle were dealt a blow a few weeks later when Bauchop broke his collarbone in a game against Southport Central but the club moved quickly to re-sign Archie Campbell as a replacement, with the side sitting fourth bottom in the table having won one, lost three and drawn two of their opening six games with just five goals for and sixteen against. The playing policy of 'short passing movement' was proving 'classier' for the spectators, if not being displayed in the results, and the side started to move up into mid-table.

United were drawn away to Coventry City in the English Cup fifth qualifying round and 6,000 saw Tickle shoot the hosts ahead after a clever dribble but Bauchop, back from his horrendous injury, levelled to take the tie to a replay which again ended 1-1, on this occasion after extra time. Sanderson shot the Cumbrians ahead following a free-kick but Warren made it all-square following a scramble from a corner. United's side was: Laburn; Ross, Carter; Blyth, Wishaw, Forster; Kirkman, Maher, Stewart, Sanderson, Bauchop. The two teams met for the third time at Manchester City's ground and United finally went through 3-1 to set up a home game against Fulham in the first round proper. United's board relented on this occasion and were talked into allowing the game to take place at Craven Cottage through a financial deal where it was rumoured they'd negotiated for £400, travelling and other expenses for a party of 25 and half of the gate money at a meeting between representatives of the two clubs at Preston. There were around 15,000 packed in at the game and United were soon three down, the goals coming from Millington, Freeman and Collins. United did better after the break but were still outclassed and Freeman got his second for number four although Bauchop did pull one back in the 75th minute with a 'pretty' goal. United had not only been knocked out, but were left grumbling about their cut of the gate money too. With the newspapers 'variously estimating the crowd at from 18,000 to 30,000, and with a 6d gate and grandstand ranging up to half a crown a seat, the receipts ought to have been more than £420.'

United were deep in financial trouble; they called an extraordinary general meeting in February where chairman Mr. C.K. Coulthard stated that 'although for the first time in the club's history the directors hoped to pay a full dividend at the end of the season,' in view of the great expenditure to be incurred on the new ground at Brunton Park the board felt that more shares would have to be taken up and they reduced the directorate qualification from £15 to £10. Mr. Coulthard said that the directors were disappointed at the return from the Fulham Cup tie but 'he would not like to impugn a club of so recognised responsible management as Fulham regarding any 'shuffling' of the receipts.' The official figure given for the attendance was between 14 and 15,000.

Mr. Nicholson of the club said he 'did not care about impugning Fulham or not: he was convinced that the gate was bigger than officially stated.'

A month later the directors were saying 'that they may have to give up the club on account of the serious financial position' and a public appeal was launched to help with the £1,000 they needed to raise to move from Devonshire to Brunton Park. United adopted a life membership scheme 'as long as the club exists' to sit in the centre stand 'on payment of £10 down' and an Advisory Committee was set up to try and steer the Blues out of trouble.

As it happened, the club's old friends across in the North East came to their rescue in their time of dire need. The directors at Newcastle United agreed to loan Carlisle £300 interest free, for three years, on the security of two shares in the new ground. Newcastle's terms were for £100 to be paid back in each year. 'This generous offer of Newcastle, supplemented with the financial aid which has been forthcoming in Carlisle district, puts the Border City club on a sound financial basis,' wrote the *Yorkshire Post*, and the *Newcastle Chronicle* noted that 'the Newcastle club have always shown a kindly disposition towards Carlisle.' The Advisory Committee had raised around £500 in promises and United's directors were responsible for the other £500 on the ground which was reputed would be 'one of the best athletic grounds in the North of England when completed.'

Although Newcastle-upon-Tyne was built on coal and Carlisle on cotton, there have long been links between the two cities - Hadrian's Wall being the obvious one. Carlisle was known as Luguvalium and was more substantial than Newcastle, which was just a bridge and Roman fort called Pons Aelius. But they are both on the frontier, the very edge of the old Roman Empire, and would remain that way for almost 1500 years as the first defence against Scottish invasion. Carlisle is just 53 miles from Newcastle, making it the closest major neighbour. It is 74 miles to Edinburgh and 84 miles to Glasgow, with Manchester being around 100 miles south.

On the pitch, the Combination side that had pulled themselves up to sixth in the table while Workington were languishing in fourteenth spot and Carlisle piled the misery on the West Cumbrians when they beat them in the Cumberland Cup Final before 4,000 spectators at Devonshire Park. Carlisle keeper Laburn produced a fantastic save to deny Laycock before United went ahead as Troughear sliced a Kirkman cross beyond his own goalie. McGraw levelled from close range just before half time but Robinson restored Carlisle's lead and Wishart added the third from a free kick. Both of the second half scorers were transferred to Sheffield United shortly after and Bauchop left to join Stockport County in the summer.

Grumbles about low gates in the North Eastern League were shown to be somewhat unfounded when Newcastle United's fixture against Sunderland pulled in a record attendance for a reserve match with 30,000 turning out to watch the Magpies win 5-1. To be fair though, only had 2,000 bothered going to watch the 'A' team beat Hartlepools United at St. James' earlier that month, so it could be very hitty-missy.

United beat the 'Pools 3-0 in one of their final North Eastern League games at Devonshire Park with Blyth putting away two penalties and Barnett netting the other after Tweddle had been fouled outside the box and one of United's final Combination games on the ground saw them beat Accrington Stanley 4-0 with Bauchop, Carter, Kirkman and Blyth on the scoresheet.

FOOTBALL SNAPSHOTS.

COLNE v. CARLISLE UNITED.

AT GRIPS IN MIDFIELD

SOUTHPORT v. CARLISLE UNITED.

1 GASKELL CLEARING FOR SOUTHPORT.
2 KIRKMAN (CARLISLE) ROBBED CLOSE IN.

Match action from January 1909.

ROVERS RESERVE v. CARLISLE UNITED

1. ROSE TO THE RESCUE.
2. BELL SAVES IN NICK OF TIME.

More Lancashire Combination action from February 1909.

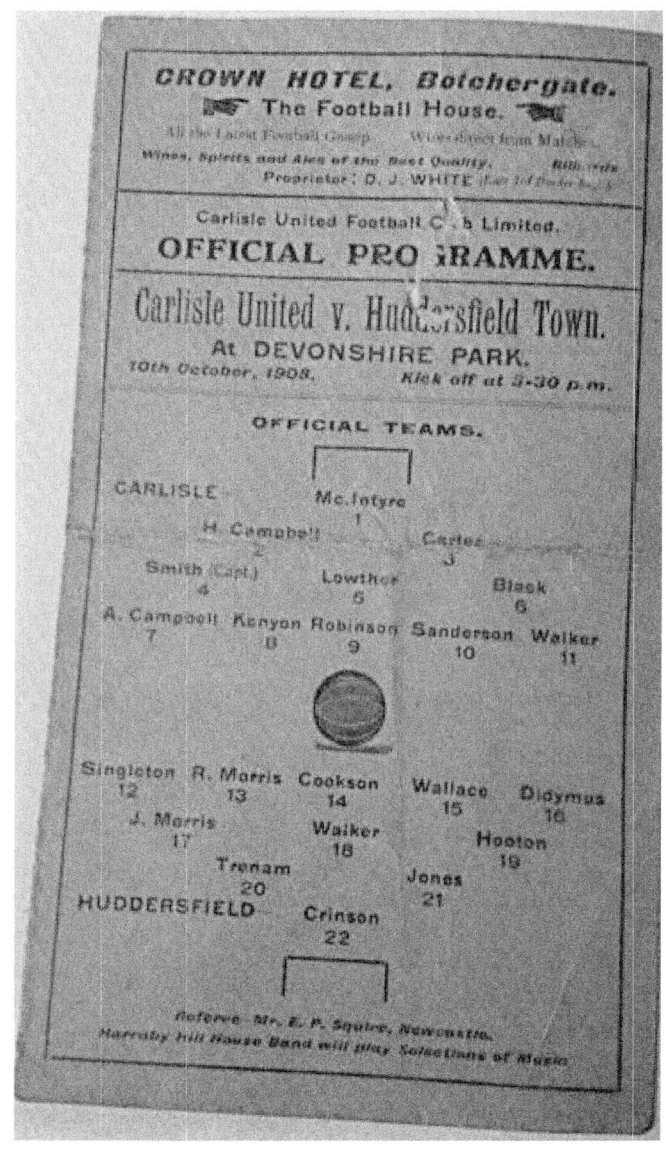

A North Eastern League programme.

11. BRUNTON PARK

THE CONCOURSE of the East Stand at Brunton Park today has a very light and spacious modern feel with its concession stands and fans milling around in small groups before taking the steps up and seeing the that magic first view of the green pitch.

With a vast high cantilever roof and stylish design, the East Stand remains one of the greatest legacies left to the club by former owner Michael Knighton – even if the travelling fans are seated away well beyond the pitch as further planned developments never happened.

The rest of the ground, however, has a much more traditional and dated ambience from the wooden seats and low, dark over-hanging roof and rabbit-warren corridors of the main stand to the bulk of grey concrete, outdoor brick bog walls and tangles of steel in the cavernous Warwick Road end terracing.

Matchdays have a feeling all of their own; people streaming down Warwick Road in blue and white scarves and hats, or Stone Island and CP Company, congregating outside the Beehive and the club shop with the bronze statue of Hughie McIlmoyle poised permanently as if he's just headed into the net with the music from the P.A. drifting off into the wind. The excitement and anticipation building as fans buy a programme and a Golden Gamble ticket then line up at the ticket offices and burger vans, the smell of boiling onions on the air. It has most likely always felt the same.

People first started walking that well-worn path past the elegant three-storey Victorian town houses on the second of September 1909 when the opening game at Brunton Park was played against Newcastle United and a report in the Athletic News on Monday 6th September reported that the first Lancashire Combination game, against Chorley, had just taken place at Warwick Road. The News noted that the new ground could hold 30,000 people and 'a substantial covered stand runs almost the full length of the pitch on one side. Excellent dressing and bath rooms, etc., are provided for the players.' A Lancashire Evening Post snippet claimed that Carlisle 'certainly played a better game than they did in their opening match against Newcastle United' but with only 3,700 at the match, and almost a good half of them travelling Chorley fans, it was probably a case of after the Lord Mayor's parade.

The Lancashire Combination side remained United's first commitment but players were appearing in both that League and the North Eastern, so the punishing fixture schedules must have put some strain on aching muscles and knocks taken during the rough and tumble nature of the game back then.

The club had brought in outside left John Law, who played for both Lincoln City and Maxwelltown Volunteers the previous season, and snapped up two more Scotsmen in goalkeeper Young from Motherwell and Phillips from Ayr Parkhouse. Makin was signed from Lancashire side Ramsbottom and the transfer activity continued with Thomas Winning coming in from Leith Athletic alongside Cooper and Greenhalgh from the Bury sides Limefield and Helton respectively and by July the probable squad for the coming 1909/10 season was looking like: Goalkeepers - T. Wilcox (ex-Manchester United and Blackpool), Young and J.A. Bell. Backs – Rose, Carter and McKenzie. Half backs – Blyth, Foster, F. Smith, Fell, Winning and Cable (former Millwall and Tunbridge Wells). Forwards – David Maher, Sanderson, W.S. Pigg, A. Barnett, Berry, Phillips, Cooper, Makin, Greenhalgh and Noble, who was captured from Glasgow Rangers, Law and Jobling, who put pen to paper from Spennymoor.

United were given permission by the CFA to enter the Lancashire Combination and North Eastern League on condition that they play their first team in the Cumberland Cup and United player T. McGarr unsuccessfully appealed a *sine die* suspension for 'failing to reveal his age when he played for Carlisle Butchers in the Shield competition.' His suspension was to remain until the end of the year. The Cumberland FA had a healthy 110 clubs affiliated and the secretary said that ten more were to be added, so the local game seemed in a healthy shape. The Carlisle & District League was in fine fettle and contained the likes of Annan Athletic, Carr's Athletic, Eskdale Juniors, Carlisle CYMS, Carlisle South End, Holy Trinity and Methodists.

United were able to announce a profit for the first

time thanks to all the financial assistance that they had received with a balance of £53 from the previous season, though the directors said that this was due to the 'satisfactory transfer fees obtained for several players.' Receipts were £3,186 and expenditure £3,133.

United began brightly in the North Eastern League with two victories on the road and one at home, with their best performance so far in a 3-1 victory over Sunderland reserves. The Blues were reputed to be 'a force to be reckoned with' in the North Eastern that season and were, although slighter in physique, 'smarter, faster on the ball and combined perfectly.' Sanderson was moved from the Combination team and tried at centre half, with the experiment proving a great success as he netted 'two grand goals.' United drew 2-2 with Middlesbrough at Brunton Park with Carter firing home a penalty to give United the lead. Dixon shot past Young to equalise and the same player had a big part to play when 'Boro notched a disputed second, racing clear with Carlisle claiming offside and Burton tucking the rebound into an empty net after the keeper parried. Carter slotted away a second penalty to make it all square.

The Combination side had also made a superb start and topped the table in an unbeaten start with wins over the likes of Manchester City and a creditable draw at Anfield and by mid-October were in fourth place with three wins, four draws and two losses from their opening nine games.

United were drawn away to Manchester League side Tonge in the fourth qualifying round of the English Cup and were confident of avoiding a potential banana skin, especially when the tie was re-arranged to Brunton Park. However, a side that lined up: Young; Rose and Carter; Blyth (capt), Martin and Foster; Jobling, Maher, Makin, Sanderson and Law just managed to scrape through 1-0 and set up a game away to Yorkshire outfit Mexborough Town in the fifth qualifying round. Town had beaten Doncaster Rovers in the previous round, so were no mugs; they didn't hand over home advantage this time and were rewarded with a 0-0 draw. United breathed a sigh of relief as they won the replay 4-0 to set up a huge game against West Ham United at Upton Park in the first round proper.

United had beaten Glasgow Rangers 6-2 at Brunton Park in a New Year friendly with Carter (pen), Maher, Sanderson, Makin and Law (2) all on target, so confidence was high in the Carlisle camp ahead of their trip to the busy East End of London in English football's premier competition.

A crowd of 11,000 watched Carlisle scrap to a 1-1 draw thanks to a penalty smashed in left-footed just under bar in the last ten minutes by the ever-reliable Carter and the game was replayed, by arrangement (financial, of course), at West Ham on the Thursday with Carlisle staying down in the capital for a few days. The Blues on this occasion went down 5-0 in front of between 6 and 10,000 in a game 'that deteriorated and became so rough that the referee had to administer several cautions.' The Cup dreams were over for another season but had brought a glamour tie down in the South and again put some much-needed cash in the club coffers.

When Carlisle headed back home from the bright lights of London (or the seedy backstreets of the tough East End – take your pick) to the bread and butter of League football they'd slipped down to tenth in the Combination with a record of eight wins, eight defeats and five draws with 45 scored and 35 conceded from the 21 games they'd played so far. Workington were struggling with just Hyde below them – and that was on goal difference. A run of victories took the Blues back up to fifth by early March with Reds pulling clear of the relegation danger zone but then soon after 'arising out of the drastic changes made by the management of the Lancashire Combination which greatly effect the two Cumberland clubs,' United's directors met at the Wellington Hotel and unanimously agreed to withdraw from the League and continue in the North Eastern the following season. They wanted a meeting with the shareholders before a final decision was taken but it was starting to increasingly look like the club's future lay towards Tyneside rather than Manchester. In fact the Geordie club was met by huge cheering crowds at both Preston and Carlisle when they returned home by train up the West Coast line with the English Cup in April, and the team was entertained by the Carlisle United directors in a stop off before getting back to Tyneside at ten minutes past six to the cheers of an estimated crowd of 150,000 at the Central Station.

When the Carlisle United shareholders met at the Queen's Hall in May, Colville Coulthard, the chairman, who resigned afterwards, said that 'the geographical change in the Lancashire Combination would rob Carlisle of their best gate-drawing teams and destroy the competitive spirit' while a new wage limit 'was impractical to a club like United.' The decision by the League had 'knocked all interest out of Lancashire Combination football at Carlisle since its adoption' and only a handful of spectators turned out at Brunton Park to watch them draw with Nelson in the final game of the season. They finished up in seventh spot level on points but ahead of Workington on goal difference.

United withdrew altogether from the Combination and decided to 'run a good team in the North Eastern and a local junior team' for 1910/11. The club was still in financial difficulties and had a deficit of £530 for the season, but 'thanks to the generosity of the Duke of Devonshire, the Earl of Lonsdale and Mr Claude Lowther, who had each subscribed £100, only £150 now remained to be raised.'

United had beaten Penrith 2-1 in a re-played Cumberland Cup semi-final with goals from Makin and Sanderson in an exciting final five minutes but were beaten 3-1 after extra time in a replayed final by Workington.

James Wishart returned to the club from Sheffield United and captain Billy Blythe, formerly of Preston, became United's longest serving player when he put pen to paper on a new deal for the coming season along with Davy Maher. The Blues then captured outside right James Maxwell, a former Kilmarnock, Sheffield and Woolwich Arsenal star who had received a Scottish International League cap aged 20, and he was joined by former Glasgow Celtic player W. Semple from Millwall and A. Beney from Arsenal as the Blues continued to build a strong side. There were departures from Brunton Park as well, though, with Tom Sanderson leaving for Chrorley and manger James Stansfield, who was aged 35, going to take up the reigns at Norwich City where he was dubbed 'the quiet man who knows' by the Canaries supporters.

The club's finances faced further strain when around £100 was spent improving the ground's drainage but the side to compete in the North Eastern was taking shape; Thomas McDonald, a goalkeeper, came from Motherwell, right back Robert Craig signed from Celtic, James Hullock came from Wallsend, James Greenham from Stockport County and four amateurs – W.S. Pigg, J. Taylor, T. Bowie and I. Robson joined those above.

United in action at Nelson in 1910.

An early image of Brunton Park.

12. LIQUIDATION

THE NORTH EASTERN LEAGUE in 1910/11 was comprised of the reserve sides from the big Football League teams Newcastle United, Sunderland and Middlesbrough alongside teams such as South Shields, North Shields Athletic, Hartlepools, Darlington, Spennymoor, Wallsend Park Villa, Seaham Habour, Hebburn Argyle, Wingate Albion, Sunderland Royal Rovers, Shildon Athletic and West Stanley, with the two Cumbrian sides and newcomers Jarrow Croft, an amateur team.

United dominated in the season opener against Wallsend Park Villa at Brunton Park but missed a number of chances as they went down 2-1. United 'delighted in the tricky and beautiful game' whereas the visitors were more direct and 'whenever they got within shooting range they had a 'pot.' Maxwell netted an equaliser and United had a great chance to get it back to 2-2 in the last minute, but Maher sent a tame shot wide from five yards with just the keeper to beat, no doubt to great groans from the wooden grandstand. Although they then drew a blank in a goal-less draw at Hebburn Argyle, United brought in a new Scottish forward called McNish who had moved to Newcastle and was playing for Heaton Avenue, and he had impressed enough during the game to earn a contract.

Carlisle then took a point off Newcastle United A in 'one of the most exciting encounters that had been seen in the Border City for some time.' Blyth scored the opener for a Carlisle side that was somewhat depleted by injuries with Allan levelling just sixty seconds later as the club began the campaign fairly brightly and full of optimism.

Striker Beney started to find his form and netted in a defeat at Newcastle then hit both goals in a 2-0 success over Hebburn before United thrashed defending champions Spennymoor United 4-1 at Brunton Park where he again bagged a brace, with Maxwell and Maher getting the others. Anthony Carter resigned for the side who were then well beaten at Hartlepools United's Victoria Ground and another Scotsman was recruited to the team, McDougall from Kirkcudbright.

With United in twelfth position in the North Eastern League, they pulled off something of a surprise in the English Cup fourth qualifying round when they won 3-0 at Newburn. Sanderson 'flashed in a lightening shot' for the opener and Beney added two more to his increasing tally after the break, with Carlisle 'taller, cleverer and better trained.' The Blues drew one-all at Crewe Alexandra with Wishart outstanding in the fifth qualifier but went out 4-3 in the replay, despite dominating the opening stages and racing into a two-nil lead with goals from Beney and Sanderson. Alexandra hit back and King beat United keeper McDonald twice in quick succession to pull it level. Maher restored United's lead but they were pegged back by Chapple. The tie went to extra time and United had a great chance to win it with ten minutes to go as they were awarded a penalty. Blyth took it, but drilled straight at keeper Coventry then lashed the rebound wildly over the bar. Crewe were awarded a spot kick at the other end after Moore had handled and King made no mistake, completing his hat-trick and dumping Carlisle out of the prestigious competition. The players were no doubt gutted that they'd missed out on the chance to take on one of the big League sides and the directors cursing the fact that they'd missed out on a big pay day with a trip to First Division outfit Bristol City awaiting the winners in the first round proper.

United hosted Workington on Boxing Day in the Cumbrian derby and took the points and local bragging rights with goals from Maxwell and Beney in front of a large crowd before the Blues earned a creditable point from Middlesbrough A at Ayresome Park, McNish shooting them ahead but W. Carr beating McDonald after the break to equalise. A defining feature of United's team seems to have been their impressive 'tricky and beautiful' midfield play but it was tempered with a lack of ruthlessness in front of goal during the period as report after report praise the style of football that the club was playing, no doubt due to the Scottish influence, with North of the Border being noted for the 'scientific' game. The style may have been pleasing on the eye, but it wasn't bringing in great results either on the pitch or through the turnstiles; United were languishing in fifteenth out of 18 clubs by the end of January, having won just four and drawing five of their 21 North Eastern League fixtures. Rivals Reds were in seventh with nine wins and three draws and when the two clubs met again at Workington in April in front of just 2,000 fans, the West Cumbrians ran out 1-0 victors thanks to a twentieth minute goal from Robson.

United slumped to a 2-1 defeat at amateurs Jarrow Croft with Chrisp netting a consolation but more worryingly, at the AGM in May, Carlisle United were wound up as the directors resigned and refused re-nomination. The club had debts of £200 and a £300 mortgage and while United had reduced the wage bill to £1,384 19s 2d, the total expenses for the season ran at £2,332 5s 3½ d with income at £2,047 including the gate money of £1,213. A report stated that 'the chief cause of the club's bad financial position is the falling-off of the attendance at matches.' United were in dire straights again and withdrew from the North Eastern League while proposals to run an amateur team received no support. It looked like it could be all over.

But through the darkness came some light – after a number of meetings, although Carlisle United as a limited company had gone into liquidation, by August the club was reconstituted on its original basis, the model adapted by the old Shaddongate club, of being managed by an annually elected committee.

Workington weren't as fortunate. The Reds also folded at the end of the season but the ominous signs had been there since January when the club had granted free transfers to six regular players – Carter, McNairn, Gain, Ellis, Woods and Lawrie – and in June the club went into liquidation with debts of between £1,500 and £1,600, 'of which nearly £1,000 was personally guaranteed by the directors at the bank, 14 directors being bound for £70 each.'

The rural isolation of Cumberland from the main centres of population and the hot-beds of football were clearly putting a massive strain on the Senior game financially and it would be ten long years before Workington were reformed.

13. REBIRTH

UNITED'S NEW OFFICIALS were disappointed, 'very sore' in fact, when former striker Bobby Tait chose to sign for Cowdenbeath instead of returning to Brunton Park from Motherwell after it had been announced that the old Lancashire Combination hit-man was on his way back to join the side which was reputed to have gathered together some thirty players ahead of the new season.

The Blues had been re-admitted to the North Eastern League after putting their affairs in order, though further details of the bail-out are sketchy at best. The League had been extended to twenty clubs on a motion proposed by Mr. McCumisky of the club at the League meeting when Carlisle had resigned, with Gateshead and Newcastle City joining the ranks – though with Workington dropping out, it was reduced to nineteen.

A solitary penalty kick was enough to see off new

boys Gateshead at Brunton Park as United opened the new season with a win and the Blues followed this up with a 3-2 success at Sunderland Rovers with the familiar names of Sanderson and Maher, along with an un-named third player getting on the scoresheet, so some of the old faces were at least still around the club. It was to prove a false dawn as United crashed to six defeats and a draw in their next seven games to sit fourth bottom in the table and confidence was low for the important clash against Accrington Stanley in the English Cup fourth qualifying round, where they were duly dumped out. The slump continued with a 5-1 mauling by Hebburn Argyle and a 1-0 defeat by Jarrow Croft but there was at least some joy for United's reserve side as they lifted the Carlisle Charity Shield with a 4-1 win over Border Depot. The reserves were competing in the Carlisle & District League against the likes of Hudson Scotts, Brampton, Adult School, St. Cuthbert's, St. James's, St. Bedes, Mortons, St. Ann's, Brampton, Eskdale, L & N.W. Temp, Carrs Athletic and the YMCA with a mix of works, church and community sides all taking part in the amateur competition.

The first team took a leaf from their book and turned things around with a confidence boosting 3-2 win over Sunderland. Robinson shot Carlisle ahead and keeper Parker saved a penalty from Sunderland's Hall before Robinson chalked up a second. Morrison tucked away a second penalty for the visitors and Hall levelled but Musgrave put a smile on Carlisle faces with the winner. It didn't last long, however, as they were then thumped 5-1 in front of a good turnout at Spennymoor despite taking a second minute lead through Neale. Foster and Musgrave netted at Gateshead, but the hosts again netted five times with United finding the North East sides just too hot to handle. Routledge struck twice against North Shields Athletic on a frost-bound Brunton Park but the visitors had already netted three times. There was at least some respite in a goalless draw at Wingate Albion but Carlisle were still fourth from bottom near the end of February with just six wins and three draws from their 23 fixtures with 30 scored and 60 conceded. It could have been worse - bottom side Sunderland Rovers hadn't won a single game and had drawn just four with a bumper 82 crashed into the back of their net. Although the 1911/12 season had been a nightmare with United landing just 20 points and ending up third bottom after losing 23 of their 36 fixtures, winning seven and drawing six, scoring only 37 and letting in 98, the City at least still had a side and that was something to build on – and United's reserves won the Carlisle & District League, finishing nine points ahead of the runners-up Eskdale. But clearly things would have to change if the Blues were to compete at the Senior level and although they started the 1912/13 season with a resounding 6-1 home defeat by South Shields, with a new player named Bowerbank netting, they then beat Newcastle City and then drew with Wallsend with the newspapers noting that they 'wcrc a greatly improved side.' The strengthening continued when the Blues signed two famous Scottish amateurs from Queen's Park in George Ramsey and Bob MacKenzie, who had appeared for an Irish amateur International team. The improving Blues beat Jarrow 4-1 at Monkton with Bell and Bowerbank both bagging doubles but after eight games it was only their second victory – five of the others ending in defeat.

United were drawn against Barrow in the fourth qualifying round of the English Cup and again were left red-faced with a first-time exit as they went down

4-1.

A 4-0 Boxing Day victory over new side Houghton Rovers at least brought some festive cheer and a big crowd watched Spottiswood and Kidd net in the first half and Bell added another after the break with 'the home team rarely appearing in better form.' The fourth scorer wasn't named.

United then slipped to a 3-2 defeat by Gateshead at Brunton Park but took the lead after good play from Spottiswood set up Sanderson to score. The 'Heed levelled through Surtees and Boyle added a second. Bell equalised for the Blues but a long-range shot from Hogg won it for the Tynesiders.

Bell was on target again twice and Bowerbank got the other in a 3-2 Cumberland Cup first round success over Workington Central, a side formed in the wake of the demise of Reds, and they started to find their form in the League as well, demolishing bottom side Wingate Albion by five clear goals – they were still rooted at third bottom however, with a record of five wins, one draw and 15 defeats with the defence leaking 71 goals. Only Gateshead, just above United, had conceded more with 75 finding the back of their net.

While the North East sides were proving a tough proposition, United pulled their socks up and moved up to 14th spot with a final record of 12 wins, 5 draws and 21 defeats with 61 for and 98 against and the junior side won the Carlisle & District League for the second successive season but it was much tighter this time, taking the silverware on goal average from Eskdale Juniors. They had, however, been deducted two points for fielding an ineligible man. The League was reduced somewhat with just Dalston Black Reds, Penrith, Carrs Athletic, Border Depot, Hudson Scott's Athletic and Catholic Y.M.S the other sides competing.

The committee running the club had been very quiet with little news appearing in the press but in June they held their AGM and 'regretted that the first three months of the campaign had been bad from both a financial and playing point of view,' but their luck had changed at the turn of the year and were reasonably pleased with their lower mid-table position in the North Eastern League. The club had a balance of £52 at the start of the season and they'd increased it to £66 by the end. In modern terms that's something like £5,000 so when you consider that the wage bill when the limited company folded was over £1000 that would be more than £61,000 at a time when the average worker's take home pay was about 20 shillings, or £70 a week.

Mr. C. K. Coulthard was elected president, Mr. J. Kidd secretary and Mr. J. Kirkpatrick assistant secretary. The treasurer was Mr. G.M. Ellis and the committee were re-elected with the addition of a Mr. McMaster. There was a discussion about the price of admission to North Eastern League games which was adjourned to be discussed at a later public meeting.

The cost of entry was obviously a bane to some Carlisle folk and a ghost started prowling the misty streets and pubs under evening gaslight; with United struggling some people must have got together and on the 18th April 1913 the *Hawick News and Border Chronicle* carried a simple four line report on a match played at Newcastleton the previous Saturday. Hearts of Liddesdale had hosted – and beaten 3-1 – a team called Shaddongate United. Whether it was a serious move to try and revive the old club as a competitor to United we'll never know as the name doesn't appear in the records again. It didn't seem to unduly perturb the officials at Brunton Park and United started to move into the transfer market again ahead of the

1913/14 season by signing John Bell and James Robinson from Longtown, a local lad called Frank Porter who had been playing for Preston North End reserves and goalkeeper William Potter from Gateshead while the 20-year-old regular Joseph Spottiswood earned himself a dream move and left to join Manchester City. United were sweating as they hadn't resigned captain W. Blyth in mid-August with the new campaign fast approaching but they had retained the bulk of the old side with Steel, Bell, Bowerbank, Irving, Kidd, Maher and McGuire remaining and James Lawrie coming in from Blantyre.

Wingate had resigned from the North Eastern League and were replaced by Blyth Spartans and United began the season with a 2-0 defeat at North Shields Athletic, Turnbull heading in the opener and Vincent adding a second before the break for the Robins in front of a modest crowd.

A bigger draw of 2,000 turned out at Roker Park to see United's R. McGough drive the heavy leather ball in from distance and W. Forster added a second with Lane pulling one back for Sunderland in the 70th minute. A 2-0 win over Seaham at Brunton Park maintained United's bright hopes with former Hull City forward Musgrave prominent in the forward line but captain Blyth, who had eventually put pen to paper back with the Blues, was sent off for retaliating to a kick from North Shield's player Simpson during a 3-3 draw in the return fixture at Carlisle. Irving netted a brilliant goal with McGough scoring a penalty and Forster striking the third.

The Blues captured another forward when they signed Coldstream centre forward Cockburn, who had been with Newcastle United as an amateur, and he was soon in the thick of things getting fouled on the edge of the box in an English Cup third qualifying round tie against Lowes. Blyth took the free kick and when the visitors' keeper fumbled, Sanderson was on hand to put it in the back of the net. The floodgates opened with Orr and Bowerbank both registering, Sanderson adding a second and Cockburn firing a hat-trick. The referee stopped the game at one point 'having to order one of the Lowes supporters off the ground for using bad language.'

Hopes of a decent Cup run were buoyed by the 7-1 success and a big crowd turned up at Brunton Park to see United dump old Lancashire Combination rivals Southport Central out 2-1. Mills beat the keeper to roll in the opener and although Central got back on terms when Blyth mis-kicked and Stringfellow beat Smith with a low drive. Sanderson crossed for Cockburn to net the winner in a real end-to-end encounter.

Dreams of further progression and a chance to meet one of the League sides in the first round were dashed at Glossop though. 2,000 saw United fall at the final qualifying hurdle for the third successive season despite Mills shooting them ahead after 15 minutes with them being well on top in the first half. The wheels fell off after the turnaround and goals from Stapley (2), Barnett and Thompson meant it would be a long train journey home in a quiet carriage with little but pride left to play for in the final four months of the season.

United did fare a little better than previous seasons when they secured a 13th placed finish – their best so far – with 11 wins, 10 draws and 17 defeats, the 48 goals that they scored being slightly worse and the 84 that they conceded slightly better while the Cumberland Cup Final against Egremont Town required three replays before being finally settled in favour of Egremont at Workington with a skied shot from Jacques spilling through the Carlisle keeper's hands to win it.

The committee, however, were declaring the season a success at the AGM at Queen's Hall with over one hundred packed inside. The club had an expenditure of £947 with an income of £1,086 11s 3d, including a balance of £66 brought forward. The Chairman, Mr. W.W. Doughty, said that the gate money had risen from £612 to £936 and membership cards from £19 to £41. Officials started to get paid with the meeting agreeing an honorarium of three guineas to the secretary and two guineas to the honorary treasurer.

Events away from the football field would have a huge impact on the 1914/15 season as Britain declared War on Germany on the 4th August. At the time people had no ideas of the horrors that lay ahead in the trenches in France and many thought that the First World War would be over by Christmas. The North Eastern League was all set to continue with Ashington joining to replace Seaham Harbour and United signed H. Routledge ahead of the campaign which began with a 5-1 defeat at Jarrow and didn't get much better as it went on, ending with the Blues in 17th position having been handed 23 defeats, winning 8 and drawing 7 with a bumper 108 goals being shipped before the League was disbanded in May.

The press was turning public opinion against the game with War intensifying and the casualties piling up and one remarkable report in the London Bystander in December 1914 claimed that 'by keeping from the national service hundreds of thousands of possible recruits, football is leaving free to the service of the Germans the same number of Uhlan's, Death's Head Hussars, Prussian guards and Landstrumers. British football is as valuable, almost, as is the state of Hesse or Baden-Baden; it is one her units. The

Grand Dukes of those states stand no higher in the Kaiser's favour than should the Football Association, and no German soldiers in action are more deserving of the Iron Cross than are the professional leather-kickers who keep possible British soldiers in a state of stupefied inactivity.' The black propaganda and shaming was all a bit over the top, but football was to do her bit. The entire Heart of Midlothian team, who would become known as McCrae's Battalion, volunteered to join the 16th Battalion of the Royal Scots and many of Carlisle's players would also be marching down to Carlisle Castle to join the Border Regiment and swap their Blue shirts for a khaki uniform and rifle as they went off to do battle in a quagmire churned by shellfire, tangled in barbed wire and pinned down by the constant chatter of machine gun fire.

Richard McGough was killed in action – the classy Cumbrian midfielder had impressed enough to sign for Newcastle United's first team in 1914/15 and joined up the Royal Garrison Artillery as a bombardier. Researching all the other deaths and horrific injuries sustained by players associated with the club during World War One could fill another book – suffice to say United, and Carlisle, had done their bit.

And football didn't end completely in the City during the conflict; with large numbers of women employed at the munitions works around Carlisle, they were formed into a Munitionettes team in 1917 for morale as much as anything and played games against the likes of the very successful Blyth Spartans Munitionettes at Brunton Park. The Blyth girls played in shorts, much to the horror of post-Edwardian sensibilities, while the Cumbrian lasses kept their modesty and played in their skirts.

Carlisle munitions girls in a jaunty nautical-style number.

The pitman's daughters of Blyth Spartans with their 'knees oot.'

14. AFTER THE WAR

WHEN THE WAR was over the Blues rejoined the reconstituted North Eastern League along with the reserve sides from Newcastle, Sunderland, Middlesbrough and South Shields, the Mariner's first team having been elected to the Football League.

The clubs West Stanley, Shildon, Hartlepools United, Spennymoor, Darlington, Blyth Spartans, Wallsend, Ashington, Houghton Rovers, Jarrow, Scotswood, Leadgate and Durham City made up the 18 teams.

It was a tough League in a tough industrial landscape of slag heaps and pit head wheels with hard men, miners in the main, playing in the squads and the open green spaces of the football pitch must have provided a much needed respite from the blackness of the coal seams dripping water six miles out deep under the North sea.

The grounds, with advertisements painted on the corrugated roofs, backed tightly onto rows of colliery terraces and the ash steps were packed with blokes in flat caps smoking cigarettes.

United had been revived at a well attended meeting in June 1919 where it was decided to continue in the North Eastern and the various County competitions that the club had competed in before the War and at a meeting of the County Association they regretted that a member of the Council, Mr. G.A. Monk, of Penrith, had been killed in action in France. The country was trying to return to some sort of normality and football would be central to that, so it was probably with some sense of relief that the administrative machine got going and the first fixtures starting to arrive on the secretary's doormats in July with United drawn away to Wigton Harriers in the preliminary round of the FA Cup. The Carlisle & District League was also back in operation and was bigger and better with sides like Eskdale, Carlisle N.E.R, Wigton Harriers, Carlisle Y.M.C.A, Dalston, Cowan Sheldons, Carlisle L & N.W.R, Carlisle Tyers, Hudson Scotts, Wigton Throstles, St. Ann's, Denton Star, Penrith, Eden Vale, Carlisle Police, Carlisle C.Y.M.S and the Brunton Park side's reserves taking part.

United's first game back in the North Eastern after the four year break would see them pitted against Houghton at Brunton Park and it was reckoned that 'an excellent team has been got together and several old players of the club have again signed on, notably H. Routledge, who performed so well with the Caledonian Loco last season.' The Blues were expecting a successful season and there must have been an excitable atmosphere in the ground but nothing could prepare the spectators, players or officials for the terrible tragedy that would occur on the pitch on the opening day.

United keeper Robert Barnes, a miner from Seaton Delaval, went up to catch a cross and collided with Houghton's Frederick Churchill, another pitman, as he attempted to head the ball. Barnes said he felt his knee touch something soft and as both players fell to the ground, the keeper flung himself to one side as not to fall on his opponent. After a time Churchill was able to walk off the field with assistance, but said he felt very ill. The Carlisle linesman was a man called Ernest Brown, a fitter, and he said the game was one of the cleanest he had ever seen with no foul play while spectator John Steel of Kendal Street gave first aid to the player before he was taken to the infirmary. Churchill died on the Thursday after two operations with a perforation of the intestines, heomorrhage and slight peritonitis. To survive four years through one of the bloodiest wars in history and then die on a football field just seems so unfair. The jury at the inquest returned a verdict of accidental death, adding that no-one was to blame, but one can only imagine how terrible the goalkeeper Robert Barnes felt.

For the record, the game ended 1-1 but the result hardly mattered. Birrell had a shot deflected into his own net by a defender for Carlisle's goal and the visitor's Fullthrope netted a penalty leveller just before the end.

The incident must have been playing on Carlisle's minds and they made a few changes to the side to visit Spennymoor United with former Liverpool reserve Frederick Colley coming in at centre half to replace Brown and G. Doyle taking Rochester's left back position. Captain Routledge moved to centre forward to make room for Spottiswood at inside left, but United crashed to a heavy 5-0 defeat. Further changes were made the following week for the return fixture against Spennymoor and although there was an improvement, there was 'again a lack of combination' as they went down 2-1.

United signed Newcastle United's South African-born back Tony Whitson, who had appeared regularly for the Magpies in the First League before WW1 and had been gassed during the conflict, soon after an easy 8-1 victory over Wigton Harriers in the FA Cup qualifier. Nanson hit four, Smith two and the others were netted by Robson and Bowerbank.

The Blues were at it again in the next round with a 6-1 drubbing of Cleator Moor Celtic – but they had to come from behind after a slow start. Snaith, Kirkpatrick, with a penalty, Bowerbank and a Smith, with a hat-trick, were on target.

Carlisle had suffered some inglorious Cup exits before the War and must have felt that they were in with a chance of a decent run after the two resounding victories; and when they were handed Frizington Athletic in the next round, they must have been secretly rubbing their hands in glee. Frizington had beaten United 3-1 in the competition at the same stage in 1914/15, as the papers duly noted, but the Blues seemed a much stronger side now and so it proved with a solitary goal enough to set up a fourth qualifying tie against Barrow, with Kirkpatrick also firing a penalty wide during tight game.

Chances were also at a premium as United were held 0-0 in the South Lakes and were without Whitson, who was replaced by Lambert, but went ahead in the replay when Kirkpatrick slammed a shot against the crossbar and Ward put away the rebound. Watson struck a second after the break to seal it but United disappointingly went out 3-1 at South Liverpool in the fifth qualifying round.

Carlisle met Ashington twice in a week over the festive period and continued their winning ways in the League with a 2-1 win over the Northumbrians at Brunton Park, inflicting only a third defeat on the Portland Park side. Kirkpatrick drilled a low shot into the corner of the net to put Carlisle ahead and although Robinson levelled, Ward produced a fine solo effort to win it. When the Cumbrians visited 'the world's largest coal mining village' a week later, the black and white's turned the tables with Grey and Clark netting before Ward pulled one back.

United were also beaten 2-1 by Durham City with Kirkpatrick again on target before goals from R. Thompson and Musgrave handed City the two points but a 3-0 victory over South Shields reserves saw the Blues in thirteen spot at the turn of the year with six wins, seven defeats and a draw.

United's reserves were still prominent in the local game and lined up: Cooper; Doyle, Campbell; Gordon, Foster, Flemming; Robinson, Parker, Park, Morley and Simpson for a Cumberland Cup first round tie at Lowca later in the month. After disposing of them, United narrowly beat Arlecdon 1-0 with a goal from Starkey before Frizington Athletic gained some revenge for their FA Cup exit by knocking the Blues out.

The first team's decent displays continued as Ward shot Carlisle ahead at Blyth Spartans but the hosts hit back with strikes from Stainsby and Gregson. United won by the same scoreline in the reverse fixture the following weekend with Kirkpatrick and E. Ward again beating the goalkeeper before one of the biggest gates of the season turned out at Brunton Park to see United beat leaders Newcastle United reserves on a drizzly day where the Blues' keeper Stoneham allow the greasy ball to spill from his grasp for the opener.

Carlisle stormed back with Watson netting a penalty and Kirkpatrick and Robinson adding to the score before the break, the Blues eventually running to a 'well deserved' 5-2 success with Ward bagging a brace.

It proved a high point as United ended the season in 13th spot with 12 wins, 3 draws and 19 defeats with 47 goals for and 76 against, but they were no doubt just happy to be back playing the game and the club's finances had again showed an improvement with a profit of almost £180. The club had taken over £3,000 in gate receipts – on which they had to pay an 'entertainment tax' of £891 19s 9d. Having fun could be a costly business and the club would need that cash as the following 1920/21 season would prove to be a pivotal one in the development of Carlisle United from their humble beginnings as Shaddongate.

R. McDOUGALL.

United's pre-War star Robert MacDougall, who went on to play for Liverpool.

15. BACK TO THE BOARDROOM

WILLIAM JAMES 'BILL' HENDERSON was a Denton Holme lad who had turned out for the Robert Ferguson schoolboys' team and while he was serving in the Border Regiment during the War he played in the Battalion team that won the Mandalay Cup across in India.

When Bill was demobbed he signed up with Carlisle United as a centre forward where he was noted for his speed and clever opportunism in front of goal and he impressed enough to earn himself a £1,000 move South to Arsenal in September 1921.

Bill spent a couple of seasons at Highbury before transferring to Southampton, where his tricky and unorthodox dribbling skills won him the nickname 'Tishy' after a famous racehorse at the time. He came home to the Border City and United after a spell at Coventry in 1928 before retiring in 1930 and running a tobacconists shop until his untimely death in 1934 aged just 37.

It's pretty safe to assume that a young Bill had probably gone along to watch the early Blues sides, maybe taking a spot at the front of the dark wooden stand at Devonshire Park with his father or an uncle, looking on in wide-eyed wonder and trying to emulate his heroes on the playground at 'Fergies.' You can see the lads doing the same today, kicking a ball around to excited shouting or merciless jeers as one of them miss-kicks.

Bill was treading a similar same path to the Scotsman Charlie Bell who had played for United in 1913/14 and netted 30 times in the North Eastern League before signings for the Gunners. His Highbury career had been cut short by the War, where he'd joined the 17th Middlesex Footballers' battalion and rose to the rank of captain. While serving in the Army he'd met the Barrow players Gallagher, Dodds and Kenny and re-joined them in July 1920 when he put pen to paper for the South Lakes side.

As well as Bill Henderson, Carlisle signed the towering 6ft former Huddersfield half back James Dow from a Wearside League side and they got the new season off to a flying start with a 4-0 defeat of South Shields reserves. Ward was back on the scoresheet with the first and Snaith, Irwen and an own goal completed the tally 'in a creditable performance...with the standard of football displayed by both teams high.'

Tony Whitson re-signed for the club and they captured another ex-Magpie when the winger Tommy Parr came across to join up. The United side that took on Darlington in September lined up: Stoneham; Crawford, Watson; Snaith, Forbes, Smith; Henderson, Routledge, Ward, Kirkpatrick and Berrill and they played in front of a bumper 10,000 in a defeat at Middlesbrough's Ayresome Park around the same time.

With the senior game flourishing, the game at a local level was also in a healthy state and the Carlisle & District League was comprised of 14 clubs, with Carlisle Celtic and Carlisle Caledonians being new additions to the ranks of the set-up. The Celts were given a rude introduction to the League, however, with an 8-2 pasting by United's reserves while Caledonians disbanded early in the New Year.

The Football League had created a Third Division that summer which was comprised solely of Southern Clubs, so to redress the balance they proposed a Northern section for the following season with clubs from the Midland, Central, Lancashire Combination, Birmingham Combination and the North Eastern League being invited to apply.

United took a huge step forward in November when they considered the merits of stepping up into League football at a meeting where it was decided to drop the old committee system and form the club into a Limited Company again. The treasurer, Mr. Ellis, stated that joining the League would mean 'a vast increase in expenditure, and extensive alterations would have to be made to the ground.' He felt that the club could not afford the expense of running a Third League team at the time as he estimated that they would 'need a gate of £600 for each home match' – the average take through the turnstiles then being £154. The club also decided that they should purchase the Brunton Park ground, which seems a bit strange since they'd had so much trouble raising the £1,000 necessary to make the move back in 1909, so those costs must have been solely in building up the banks and grandstand, levelling the pitch and erecting the wooden perimeter fences.

On the pitch, Henderson was on the goal trail with a double in a 3-0 win over Sunderland reserves at

Brunton Park with Kirkpatrick grabbing the other and United advanced in the FA Cup by seeing off old rivals Frizington, then beating Barrow after extra time in a replay before 5,000 with Ward netting the all-important goal to set up a second qualifying round meeting with Wath Brow. Barrow, however, contested the result by claiming that United had played an ineligible player in centre-forward Craig, who had been signed the day before the date for the previous round was fixed. The FA Board upheld the appeal and the Blues were thrown out of the competition. To add insult to injury, they also had to pay the costs. Talk about a kick in the teeth.

The club made a provisional application to join the new Third Division (North) in January but the secretary, Mr. G. Bristow, said that 'they must be in a position to acquire their football field at Brunton Park before they could actually get in.'

The players were doing well on the turf and were up to seventh in the table, winning comfortably at Bedlington United 3-0 with Craig scoring twice and Henderson getting the other, then remarkably beating Shildon 4-1 with only nine men in the second half due to injuries to Snaith and Crawford.

The real test of Carlisle's mettle would be against the other clubs that had ambitions of going up into the extended Football League at the end of the season – Darlington, Ashington, Durham City and Hartlepool – United having withdrawn their application in March after raising promises to the value of just £1,200 of the £5,000 required to purchase the ground. Of the four clubs, only Darlington were above United in the table at the time so it could be reasonable assumed that United would have stood a great chance of election. The Blues had comfortably beaten Hartlepool 4-1 at Brunton Park earlier in the season and the following side: Stoneham; Routledge and Whitson, Snaith, Forbes and Kirkpatrick; Nanson, Shannon, Henderson, Kilgour and Birrell completed a double at Victoria Park in steady rain in front of just 700 odd fans. Kilgour struck the first from a corner and Henderson added a brilliant second, flicking up and heading on to race clear of the defence before beating Aldridge as he advanced off his line. Birrell added a third at the second attempt after his initial shot was blocked on a greasy pitch which cut up badly.

Towards the end of the campaign Ashington beat United 1-0 at Portland Park and the two sides drew 1-1 in the return at Brunton Park with Kilgour scoring for the Cumbrians and Hutchinson replying for the Northumbrians. Darlington were Champions but the season proved United's most successful in the North Eastern League to date as they won 18, drew 10 and lost 10 to finish a very creditable sixth.

Hartlepools finished four points behind the Blues in seventh and Ashington ended up in ninth, some five points adrift. Durham City were well off the pace in twelfth, but went into the Third Division (North) with the other three sides.

The defunct Cumberland Senior League was proposed to be revived at a meeting with representatives from the clubs Moss Bay, a revived Workington Reds, Workington DSS, West Seaton, Workington Black Diamonds, Harrington, Egremont, Maryport, Flimby and Carlisle United in attendance where there was 'a unanimous expression of opinion that it would be an excellent departure in the bettering of football in the county if such a League were formed.' United's reserves had been in a neck-and-neck battle with Penrith for the Carlisle & District title, with the 'Bonny Blues' eventually lifting the silverware, but the Reserves took the Carlisle Hospital

Cup though they went out of the Cumberland Cup in the semi-final stage against Cleator Moor Celtic.

Penrith and Wigton Harriers – both former members - indicated that they had no intentions of leaving the Carlisle & District to join a revived Cumberland League and felt that the competition had a bit of a misnomer with 'the almost entirely West Cumbrian character of the membership.' Things had been going badly in the Derwent Valley League which was felt to be due to 'the system of club representation on the league committee and consequent lax handling of clubs which place their own interests before those of the league,' so the East Cumbrian sides probably felt that they'd be better off without it, though Carlisle United were supportive of the idea.

T. WHITSON, Newcastle United.
(Photo by Stuart & Whinfield. Newcastle-on-Tyne.)

W. Henderson

Bill 'Tishy' Henderson in his Southampton kit.

16. CHAMPIONS

CARLISLE UNITED (1921) LTD, the company that controls the present club, was formed after the AGM in July 1921 at which it was announced that profits had increased from £179 to £320. It was proposed to raise £2,000 with which to purchase the ground at Brunton Park (though it had been stated at £5,000 earlier in the year?) and they had signed on sixteen players, including the backbone of the previous season's squad.

A newspaper report in the *Lancashire Evening Post* commented that 'it was agreed that the money standing to the credit of the club be handed over as a working balance to the new company, and it was announced that that the directors had under consideration a proposal to retain the old club committee as an advisory committee.' It was at that moment that Shaddongate United was really gone forever and the modern Carlisle United was born. Some of the old 'Gate players would undoubtedly have been still going about their jobs in the City, probably making their way down to Brunton Park themselves as fans in their waistcoats and jackets, getting a pat on the back from old friends and work-mates that recognised them or maybe being bought a pint – though this was now illegal under the State Management Scheme which was in operation in Carlisle's pubs. Times had changed; the focus would now be on bringing Football League matches to Carlisle.

United's first signings included John Cole, a striker from Wearside League champions Seaham Harbour and a Northern League player, Thomas Baxter. B. MacPherson, the son of Newcastle United's trainer, was also signed up along side S. Rowell from Jesmond Villa and Murphy from South Shields with the new limited liability company's management very confident of success.

Workington Reds were back and rejoined the North Eastern League 'with Workingtonians jubilant, but at the same time it is felt that a big effort will be needed to rise to the standard required for success in the League.' Darlington reserves, Preston Colliery and Seaton Delaval filled up the other three spaces left by the departure of Ashington, Darlington, Hartlepool and Durham City to the Third Division (North).

The Blues didn't make a particularly auspicious start as they were held to a goalless draw at Brunton Park by Chester-Le-Street in the season opener but they cruised through an FA Cup preliminary round tie against Barrow side Vickerstown with Ward and Henderson, in one of his last appearances before heading down to London, both netting two each and Birrell adding the other. Liverpool actually came in with an offer of £1,500 after Henderson had signed for Arsenal but the deal was done as the Gunners got Henderson employment, so it was probably what we would term a semi-pro contract today.

They were defeated by South Shields reserves but beat Chester-Le-Street 3-1 in the return League fixture as they started to find their form and carried it into the qualifying rounds of the Cup when they thrashed Penrith 6-1 and Arlecdon Red Rose 8-0 in a match that resembled a shooting practise. Ward hit two, Cob two and Kilgour two, with Fedden and Kirkpatrick also on the scoresheet. It could have been more, but United 'slackened pace later in the game.'

United drew 2-2 with Newcastle United and beat Bedlington United 3-1 with the scorers being Robinson and Ward, with another brace, in the League before seeing off Cleator Moor Celtic in the FA Cup with Cole and Spencer, from the penalty spot, doing the damage before the Blues were unlucky to go out 3-2 to Stalybridge Celtic in a replay in the final qualifying round with a visit to Third Division Hartlepools United awaiting the victors in the first round proper.

The Blues were in great form and would have fancied their chances after thumping Jarrow 5-1 with Cole, Nanson and Ward scoring in a first half blitz, then beating Seaton Delaval 3-1 thanks to a Kilgour hat-trick and Darlington reserves 7-2 with Cole this time netting a treble and Ward, Kilgour, Robinson and Birrell getting pats on the back as they jogged back after putting the others away.

It had been ten years since Carlisle had met Workington and around 7,500 turned out at Lonsdale Park on Boxing Day to see the Blues record a 3-1 victory and inflict a first home defeat of the season on their West Cumbrian rivals. A bumper 12,000 were at Brunton Park as United completed a double with a giant roar meeting Ward's opener after just two minutes. The crowd were animated again when

Kirkpatrick added number two early in the second half.

Fleming scored a late penalty to hand United's reserves the Cumberland Shield after they came from behind when Reay shot opponents Frizington Harriers ahead at Workington, but Harrison equalised and with better finishing, United could have had more.

A week later and the first team also had to stage a comeback after being two goals down at Blyth Spartans with McGuire and Herron giving the table-topping green and whites the advantage before goals from Kilgour and Ward salvaged a point.

The Blues had seen off Spartans 2-0 on News Years' Day with both goals coming from reserve inside left Nanson after being set up by Ward as the festive games kept coming thick and fast.

A surprise 4-2 defeat at Spennymoor United, with Kilgour scoring twice, put the skids on the fantastic run though a 3-1 success over Darlington reserves and a 4-1 victory over the Red Devils of Seaton Delaval put Carlisle right back in contention, although they were then held to a surprise 1-1 draw at Bedlington United with Kirtley beating Blues keeper Stoneham to cancel out Singleton's opener.

Ward and Kilgour were back in business in a 2-1 win at 'The Track,' the nickname for new-boys Preston Colliery's ground, with a 'polished and scientific style that was a treat to see' and they signed two amateurs to strengthen the squad for the run in with Walker, a left back playing in the Northern Alliance, and former Blackpool inside forward G.G. Iddon coming to the club.

By the end of February the *Shields Daily News* was noting that 'Carlisle United are making a bold bid for Championship honours in the North Eastern League this season and to all appearances their chance is an extremely rosy one, being only three points behind the leaders and having four games in hand.' People were starting to sit up and take notice and the Blues' win at the pitman's ground – being only the second club to win at Hawkey's Lane - was well received and the paper concluded by stating 'those who witnessed Carlisle's performance were greatly impressed by their splendid all-round display, and will wish them every success in accomplishing their great desire.'

United won the return game 3-1 thanks to goals from Kilgour, Ward and Robinson but the irrepressible forward line were mis-firing as they suffered a set-back with a 1-0 defeat at Shildon - Richmond grabbing the only goal in the first minute – and a valuable point was dropped when they were held by Sunderland reserves as Stannard cancelled out Ward's opener.

The Blues booked a spot in the Cumberland Cup Final by beating Moor Row at Workington with Wright on target, though they did breathe a sigh of relief when a Starkie shot cannoned back off the upright, and the Championship run-in began with a 1-0 win at Sunderland reserves when Kilgour latched onto a weak clearance by Welsh amateur International G.A. Mitchell to score before a mid-week goalless draw at St. James' Park with Newcastle's reserves left Carlisle just two points behind the black and whites, who topped the table, with two games in hand

Nerves were rattled after a hard-fought narrow 2-1 success at bottom-side Scotswood. The Westenders went ahead after just ten minutes when Robson shot home but Spencer equalised from the penalty spot and Ward grabbed the winner. It looked like Carlisle could blow it when they suffered a surprise 1-0 defeat at Jarrow but they quickly bounced back with an impressive performance to beat Spennymoor 3-0 on a

Thursday night at Brunton Park to put them top of the table by one point with both the Blues and title rivals Newcastle having just two games left to play. United maintained pole position by beating Houghton 2-0 while Newcastle were also 2-0 winners at Jarrow on the Saturday, setting up a dramatic finale.

United faced Shildon at Brunton Park in the last game of the season knowing that a win would hand them the silverware; Newcastle reserves beat West Stanley 3-1 in their game but the Blues won 2-0 and celebrated at the club's annual dinner that night.

The Mayor, Mr. A. Creighton, was present at the do and told of when the Mayoress had played in goals for the Carlisle munition girls' team back in 1917.

It was the club's most successful season to date; they'd won the North Eastern League, the Cumberland Shield, the Carlisle & District Charity Shield, and the Carlisle & District Charity Cup.

The Wigton Charity Cup Final ended in a fiasco for the reserves as during a third replay against Carlisle Eden Vale in a heavy rain storm, United's players walked off the pitch drenched after the Vale had scored and the presentation of the Cup was withheld. The reserves, in their defence, said that they Eden Vale players hadn't turned up on time and they 'were frozen to the bone' as it kicked off twenty minutes late. Two players remained on the pitch but the other nine were fined and suspended by the Cumberland FA for 'leaving the ground without permission.'

The Blues, however, clinched an important double when they secured the Cumberland Cup in a replay against Cleator Moor Celtic, thrashing them 6-0 at Workington.

Carlisle United had cemented their place as the preeminent side in the County.

A couple of North Eastern League medals from the 1920s

17. THE ENGLISH CUP

NO SIGNS REMAIN of the old Shaddongate United club in Carlisle today; they are a bit of an enigma, a half-remembered story told by grandfathers. The City itself has changed, too, the old industrial heritage replaced by plush apartments, the ramshackle Lanes in the City centre demolished and replaced by a modern shopping centre. The smoke and soot of the railway locomotives that shunted into town are long gone, the factories closed, the clatter of the mill machines silenced.

The Championship season of 1921/22 was Carlisle United's best in the North Eastern League. Club official Mr. Pattison was presented with their medals at the annual meeting of the League at the Crown Hotel in Newcastle and United treated the other team representatives that were present to a tea.

The Carlisle United Supporters Club had been formed some 18 months previously and they had paid the club around £436, for shares in the main, with other sums added by the 830 people in membership making it up to £478 and the first yearly report of the new limited company noted that the directors had successfully purchased the ground at Brunton Park. The profit margin in the balance sheet was a healthy one, too, with the club £623 in the black – no doubt helped by the transfer money for Bill Henderson. A number of improvements had taken place at the ground, much of the work being done voluntarily by the supporters club. Mr. T. Henderson, E.J. Hodgson and T. Lockhart were elected to the directorate.

The club had successfully resigned the entire championship winning side by early July and added outside right James MacKay from Coventry City and Chippenfield from Blyth Spartans ahead of the new season.

A 2-0 defeat at Darlington reserves in the opening fixture didn't auger too well but the Blues gained some redemption by beating the Quakers 3-1 in the reverse a week later with Clark, a Ward header from a MacKay centre, and a Cooperthwaite goal putting United in charge before half time at Brunton Park.

With the League games still in the main being played as back-to-back fixtures, United had Ward and Clark on the scoresheet in a 2-2 draw at Wallsend but then saw them off 3-1. United were without their experienced captain Tony Whitson and the injured Wilson as they shared a point with Hartlepools United reserves in a scoreless encounter at Carlisle and they ended the opening month with heavy defeats at both Middlesbrough and Jarrow. A lad called Warwick, from Brampton, netted two of the South Tynesider's goals in their 3-0 win. The irony wasn't missed by Carlisle and they quickly moved to snap up his signature. Warwick had netted a hat-trick in his first game for Jarrow and joined the Blues after just three games 'at his own request.' The Blues also added a big-name signing in former Tottenham Hotspur and Dundee outside right Hugh Lorimer.

Their best League performance of the season to date came in a creditable 2-2 draw at the unbeaten leaders Newcastle United with Kirkpatrick firing both into the back of the net and they again held the Magpies 0-0 in the return in Carlisle.

The FA Cup campaign began brightly with a 7-1 drubbing of Fleetwood. Cole (3), Nanson (2), Ward and Chipperfield were the scorers, but the erratic form away from home in the NE League continued when the Blues went down 1-0 at Seaton Delaval's Wheatridge Park ground, Buckham grabbing the only goal twelve minutes from time.

United hit six in their fourth qualifying round tie with the Cup proving a massive draw and 6,000 seeing Felling Colliery thumped at Brunton Park. Nanson latched onto a Birrell pass to give United a slender lead at the interval but they piled on the pressure after the break with Cole adding number two, Nanson heading in the third before drilling in his hat-trick from distance. Ward and Cole completed the scoring.

Carlisle played in something of a rarity when they were drawn away to Welsh side Aberdare Athletic, who played in the English Third Division (South), in the sixth and final qualifying round.

A crowd of 10,000 watched United gain a creditable 0-0 draw but Carlisle's interest in the competition was ended when they were defeated 2-1 after extra time in the replay. Mackay was proving a handful for the League side's defenders and Kirkpatrick went close on three occasions with long-range snapshots. Chipperfield also went close with an effort from outside the area and, although the Welshmen showed 'far better football in midfield and were more scientific in all departments' a great roar erupted in the ground as Ward headed United in front deep into the second half.

Martin grabbed an equaliser with just four minutes to go and the same player snatched a breakaway winner in extra time. There clearly wasn't a great deal of difference in the standard of the Third Division and that of the NE League and United will have been heartened, despite the defeat.

This was reflected in their League form as United went on to achieve a very creditable sixth spot with 19 wins, 8 draws and just 11 defeats all season, going a tremendous 15 games undefeated during the run-in, and they won the final game 3-1 against Leadgate Park with recent signing Duncan McDougall, formerly of Millwall, Alloa and King's Park, and Ward (2) the marksmen.

Carlisle had lost J. Mackay to Notts. County and another important player departed when goalkeeper Stoneham signed for Sunderland in May.

Work on the ground was on-going and the supporters club added additional terracing during the close season while in the boardroom Chairman Mr. W. Pattinson stated that they club had received almost 300 applications from players wanting to join the club after the secretary George Bristow, of Portland Place, put an advert in the *Athletic News* paper which read: 'Wanted. Right full back, Left half back and outside right: only first-class players need apply, giving full particulars, clubs played for, age, height, weight and terms required.'

They had already signed on a forward called Pringle who had played for the English Railwaymen's team in the N.U.R. series of International matches the previous season. Carlisle was closely linked with the railroad workers; the Carlisle & District League was packed with railwaymen's sides such as the Glasgow & SW, the London & NW and Midland. The local League also had a couple of new additions in the Holme Head and Caldew Vale clubs.

Carlisle's directors reported a loss of £250 for the season, although the gate receipts had gone up to £5,539 and the net revenue going forward was £373.

Edward Toward, of Jarrow, declined a month's trial at Tottenham Hotspur and joined the Blues and he was joined by experienced 28-year-old Scottish centre-forward Alexander Donachie from Clydebank. The Falkirk Herald noted that 'Scottish players are evidently in demand by Carlisle United' with Peter Nellies, from Hearts, Hannigan, formerly of Hibs, McDougall, and McColl all making up a strong tartan contingent at the club for 1923/24.

Hopes were obviously high as 5,000 turned out to see the first game at Brunton Park but the crowd were left grumbling (if you've ever stood in the Paddock, you'll get the general idea) as first half goals from Larnack and Wensley gave visitor's Shildon the two points.

Ward hit the only goal in the second half as Carlisle inflicted a fourth straight defeat on visitors Preston Colliery to record the first victory of the campaign and they were lucky to draw against the pitmen in the return seven days later, scoring the equaliser with almost the last kick of the game as a leg-weary defender sliced at a MacDougall centre leaving Ward with the simple task of leaving keeper Briggs helpless.

The Colliers had gone ahead when Dawson headed in a Thompson cross, the goal being 'greeted with great enthusiasm, for it was the first occasion (so far that season) that a Colliery player had managed to locate the net.'

Ward was again on the scoresheet and Donachie got the other as United recorded their second win by beating Blyth Spartans at Brunton Park but Spartans took their revenge with a 2-0 win a week later.

Ward was in hot goal-scoring form and took just sixty seconds to beat the Hartlepool keeper to a great roar from the 5,000 in the ground. Although 'Pools levelled from the penalty spot, Pringle bagged a brace and Wilson rounded things off with number four, but the inconsistencies in United's play saw them then beaten 2-1 in the reverse fixture with Ward maintaining his hot form by adding another goal to his mounting tally. The hit and miss nature of the side continued all season and meant that they finished up in a disappointing 11th spot with 13 wins, 8 draws and 17 defeats and a goal difference of minus 15.

While the League games brought in valuable gate money and kept things ticking over, it was the FA Cup competition that many regarded as the most important and Carlisle adapted their tactics better to the heavy pitch at Holker Street as they sent Barrow crashing out at the fourth qualifying round stage. Matthews had given the hosts a first half lead but Ward once again had his shooting boots on to level and Hannigan got the winner in front of an attendance of 4,000.

United's reward was a trip to old North Eastern League acquaintances Ashington, now of Division Three (North), in the fifth qualifier. The Colliers won it 2-0 and went ahead after just eight minutes as Laverick pounced when United keeper Hood parried away a shot from Gardner. Ashington, described as 'undoubtedly the stronger side' made things safe when Laverick added his second two minutes after half time, but it was a good indicator for the Brunton Park club as to the step up required to move into

League football.

United's reserve side had left the Carlisle & District League and re-joined the reformed Cumberland League with Workington Reserves, Maryport, Whitehaven Athletic, Cockermouth Town, Crosby Villa, Aspatria Athletic, Keswick and Moss Bay. Not that it had weakened the local league, by any means. The Carlisle and District now had two divisions with Penrith, Carlisle L.N.W, Brampton, Wigton Harriers, Silloth Town, Cowan's Athletic, Dalston, Upperby, Carlisle G.S.W, Eskdale, Carr's Athletic, Carlisle Midland, Wigton Throstles and Carlisle London Road in Division One and Holme Head, London Road Res., Etterby Rovers, Cummersdale, Caldew View, Carr's Athletic res., Hudson Scotts Ath., Brampton Res, G.S.W. Res, Carlisle CYMS, Carlisle St. John's and Carlisle R.F.A in Division Two. Holme Head took the Second Division title with 16 wins, 4 draws and just 2 defeats from their 22 games with a bumper haul of 112 goals and just 25 conceded.

A report was bemoaning the fact that the Cumberland FA's 'red tape' had forced a benefit match for old United favourite Billy Foster to be put off. Foster was a professional footballer, but had been playing under licence for the Carlisle C.Y.M.S club without pay. The FA 'objected to a professional who has signed to receive no remuneration getting any money from a benefit match.'

The Blues did at least have to get out the Brasso as they claimed the Cumberland Cup by beating Workington with both clubs putting out the North Eastern League sides and hot-shot Ward, of course, was the match winner with the only goal of the game from a corner.

The club had brought in John Gilchrist from Preston North End as player coach towards the end of the season, but the ex-Celtic man, who had one International cap, was off to Third Lanark. They moved swiftly into the transfer market to sign J.W. Kasher, a former Sunderland player, from Stoke, and Paul Stannard, a former Sunderland and South Shields inside right. The balance sheet issued by the board showed another £250 loss.

The days go quickly when you count your life in seasons, and another one was soon around and back into action for 1924/25. The Roaring Twenties; or the Boring Twenties, I would suspect, for anyone outside of the champagne and cocaine set in Paris, Berlin and London. There's not much glamour in sitting shivering on an outdoor netty in a cloth cap and collarless grandad shirt, cobbled streets gleaming wet with rain and the sharp tang of coal smoke drifting up from chimneys of red brick two-up, two down terraces into grey Northern skies or chucking the pigeon muck that you've scraped up off the wet ducket boards onto a Leek trench. Aye, you'd have thought you'd walked straight onto the set of a Catherine Cookson film with dirty-faced lads in oversized boots hanging around outside the grounds in little gangs back then. Football was an escape from the drudgery of daily working life, a chance to take a bit of pride in your own town and area.

18. FLOODED OUT

IT'S SEPTEMBER AGAIN and the sweet smell of cut grass is fresh in the air, a squeaky wheel on the line painting roller maintaining a steady rhythm as it runs along the tightly stretched strings to daub the tips of the blades in white lime.

The nets are hung ready from the goalposts and it's another season of possibilities; football always gives you another chance, like a lover that you keep going back to as you just can't get that lingering scent of her perfume out of your nose.

United's fans were feeling let down themselves after an opening day defeat at home by Shildon with the defence facing criticism for a 'shaky display' in the 3-1 loss, new signing Kasher the only one to come out of the game with much credit. They got things right in the meeting at the Railwaymen's ground a week later though, with Stannard unlucky not to get a hat-trick and the Shildon keeper was kept busy with further shots from Hunt and Soulsby in a 2-1 win.

The big talking point in the City and throughout the County, however, was the fact that the Blues had been drawn away to Workington at Lonsdale Park in the English Cup, with an excitable bold headline reading 'WORKINGTON AND CARLISLE TO MEET' in the *Lancashire Evening Post*. United won it 2-1 and then romped past Cleator Moor Celtic 5-1 in the next qualifier, though the newspaper report claimed that the West Cumbrians didn't deserve such a drubbing as 'Carlisle took their chances and Cleator did not.'

United signed a new full back named E. Watson from Sunderland West End ahead of the next qualifier against Egremont. Watson had formerly been with Rochdale and Queen's Park Rangers and was a ex-schoolboy International. United swept Egremont aside and drew Northern League team Bishop Auckland in the fourth qualifying round.

Bishops were famous as winners of the FA Amateur Cup on four occasions, the last time being in 1921/22, and would prove no walkover for the Blues. They were probably bitterly disappointed to go out in front of 6,500 fans at Brunton Park though, as the amateurs scored with their only shot on goal by Donald in the fifteenth minute.

With hopes of a Cup run over for another year, the Blues would have to put all their efforts into the NEL - but the club were taken to almost the brink of financial ruin in early January 1925 by a now-all-to familiar natural disaster as the Eden burst its banks and the floods wrecked the ground. In a frightening precursor to the torrents that engulfed Brunton Park in both 2005 and 2015, a bank of brown water came gushing over and caused damage estimated at between three and four hundred pounds.

The club had begun the season with a bank overdraft of £750, which had been reduced to around £350 over the first three months of the season. Mr. Nicholson, the vice chairman of the club, pointed out that Carlisle had 13 away matches still to play in the NEL where no gate money would be coming in and the cost of taking the club to the games was estimated at around £250. The directors felt that the club would be about £900 down by the end of the season and while the authorised share capital of the club was £5,000, only £1,500 had been subscribed. Chairman Mr. Theodore Carr offered to finance 200 £1 shares, allowing the shareholders to pay back in instalments, so that the repair work on the battered ground could begin immediately.

Reports paint a horribly fresh-in-the-memory picture of devastation throughout the City; Caldewgate was under several feet of water with shop goods floating in the street, Carr's biscuit factory was flooded out and 'large crowds gathered and gazed bewildered at the sight.' People took refuge in the upper rooms of their houses with the basements flooded out and left their furniture to rot in the water. A report in *The Scotsman* said 'the scene was unprecedented in the history of the city and the flooding of the houses struck terror into the hearts of the people...the flood was the worst in the memory of the oldest Carlisle inhabitant.'

Remarkably the club seem to have been back on the ground within a couple of weeks, beating Spennymoor United 2-1 on the road then securing a win over Darlington by the same scoreline, Ruddy netting twice on what must have been a sodden, heavy pitch – though contemporary reports make no mention. The Blues had played 18 games and won 11 at this stage, losing only five, but their form unsurprisingly seemed to take a bit of a nosedive after the trauma of seeing the City underwater had sunk in and they dropped away to finish the season in eleventh spot again, losing eleven of their remaining twenty games and winning just five more.

Stannard hit his 21st goal of the season in a 1-0 win at Wallsend in late January and he added number 22 in another slender victory over South Shields at home a week later before a new forward called J. Manly was signed from Craghead United as cover for the injured Lenny.

The floods don't seem to have had too much of an effect on the Carlisle & District League, who were getting through their games with two new additions to the Second Division – South Tyne Rangers from Haltwhistle and Gretna from just over the Border.

Holders United fielded a reserve side at Workington in the Cumberland Cup where they went out 3-1 and two of their old players, Reed and Reynolds, were back in first team action in a defeat at Chester-le-Street as the injuries piled up. Inside right Soulsby had broken his leg in the derby game with Workington on New Year's Day and a hand collection for him raised £17 10s.

United's form may have been poor from February onwards but they pulled off a surprise 1-0 win at Newcastle United in the penultimate game of the season and more importantly the club were able to report just a small financial loss on the season despite having to fork out over £300 on the ground repairs and hoardings. The club did withdraw from the Cumberland League, however, on account of the 'disappointing financial results.' United had, quite literally, weathered the storm.

The Blues were excluded from the preliminary round of the FA Cup in 1925/26 and would go straight into the first round proper. West Cumbrian rivals Workington were also put straight into the first round draw as the NEL clubs received a boost in standing from the FA.

Carlisle had almost completed their team building for the new season by adding two new wingers, Charles Marston coming in from Bury and William Younger from Seaton Delaval. The probable side was looking like: Goal: R.R. Hoods, Backs: J. Smiles and E. Watson. Half-backs: M. Reid, T. Loughran, and C. Wilson; Forwards: Marston, P. Donaghy, P. Stannard, W. Ward, W. Younger. Other players signed on at the club were a local lad Sid M. Cooper and M. Kirkpatrick. Loughran came to the club from Sunderland West End and Donaghy had been at Middlesbrough. Brown also put pen to paper with the Blues – he'd formerly been with South Shields and Cardiff and joined from Luton, with the newspapers boasting that United would 'have one of the strongest sides they have had since they joined the NEL.'

The reserves re-joined the Carlisle & District League and in a funny little sideline a rabbit ran onto the Brunton Park pitch during a second-string game 'having evidently strayed from the adjoining fields and gained free admittance through the 'popular side's' turnstile.' Spectators chased it *Benny Hill*-style around the embankment until it was grounded by a dog and, not quite so humorously for the rabbit, 'caught and killed by a boy.'

It probably went in the pot as socially times were tough, especially in the NEL region. A crowd were heard singing the 'Red Flag' outside Gateshead police court that month when 52 out-of-work Chopwell miners were charged with stealing coal. There are two streets in former mining village named Marx and Lenin Terrace and the faces of both revolutionaries featured on the militant pit's Lodge Banner along with Keir Hardie.

The Communist Party had an office on Globe Lane in Carlisle among the tightly packed back streets of

The Lanes in the centre of town and Shaddongate's first game against a senior side, the Association or City club, had been to help contribute to the funds of striking trade unionists – they had been very much a working-class side and the sport was long known as the working man's game. The National Union of Railwaymen in the City had paralysed travel on the rails between Carlisle and Newcastle in early 1924 with strikes and they also had a canny football team – they'd reached the final of the NUR's National Orphan Fund Competition a year previously.

The Union held annual conferences at the Crown and Mitre in the City during these tumultuous times with Carlisle being a major rail centre. The bulk of the sides in the league, however, were centred around coal mining communities – Preston Colliery, Seaton Delaval, Blyth Spartans, Bedlington United and Annfield Plain being especially linked to the pits.

South Shields reserves got the train over for the opening game at Brunton Park and although Ward was on target for the Blues against the Mariners the visitors pulled off a surprise with replies from W. Smith, Guyan and Henderson and then the side, which lined up Hood; Smiles and Watson, Kirkpatrick, Bertram and Wilson; Stott, Donaghey, Stannard, Ward and Younger went down 5-0 at Newcastle United reserves with Loughlin netting a treble and Dowsey getting the other two.

With the big name signings appearing in the first team, a number of familiar local names featured in the Carlisle club's Cumberland Shield side which at the time was Graham; Bonner, Harkins; Hetherington, Troughear, T. Telford; Hullock, Monaghan, Fyfe, J.H. Telford and Hewson. They were beaten by the railwaymen's L.N.W. side, which contained former United player Harold Brown, in an early Carlisle &

District League fixture that term.

Ward was again the scorer with what proved the match-winner against Middlesbrough reserves and he added another, with Bertram also on the scoresheet, in a victory at West Stanley as Carlisle started to find their form in what was to prove a hugely improved season.

United carried their decent League displays into the FA Cup and sent Workington Reds out 3-1 in November with goals from Cooper, Younger and Ward, with Charlie Wilson and keeper Hood outstanding. Hopes of further progression were high but the Blues suffered an ignominious first round exit at home to Northern Alliance side Chilton Colliery on a frozen pitch a couple of weeks later which also saw two of the leading players badly injured. Bertram had to be carried off the pitch with a deep gash above his right eye after just 23 minutes and Crone fractured his shoulder in the moments approaching half time.

Sheppard shot the amateurs ahead against the nine men from the penalty spot and Scurr fired the second into the back of the net a few minutes from the end, Chilton being 'more balanced and quicker on the ball than their professional opponents.'

United met Workington in the NEL derby at Lonsdale Park on Boxing Day and went ahead through Stannard but the Reds turned things around with goals from Scullion and Shaw to inflict a first league defeat since the end of October, though the Blues gained their revenge in the return fixture on New Year's Day as Cooper hit the only goal in a game where there was 'never a dull moment.'

United crashed out of the Cumberland Cup at Maryport – the same side that had done for them in the Shield – but it was small fry as at a meeting of the club on the evening of Thursday 25th March 1926 'it was decided to instruct the directors to consider the advisability of applying for membership of the Third Division (Northern Section) of the Football League.' A report in the Lancashire Evening Post said that the directors had 'come to the conclusion that not only are the prospects of success quite reasonable, but also that the step would be justified by the amount of support which would be forthcoming.' United, it seemed, were ready for the big time.

They tested themselves with a club match (a friendly) against Halifax Town, who ended up in fifth spot in Division Three (North) that season, and must have been greatly encouraged by a 1-0 win courtesy of a 'rasping shot' by Hamilton.

Back in the League United thrashed Bedlington United 6-1 at Brunton Park despite going behind in the first minute to a Banks goal. Stannard, Ward and Cooper all bagged braces and they completed their fixtures with a 2-1 victory over Annfield Plain thanks to goals from Cooper and Ward. The Blues finished up in fifth spot with 19 wins, 9 draws and only ten defeats all season.

United and Blyth Spartans, who had twice before unsuccessfully applied for admission, were the two NEL clubs seeking to get into the Northern Section of the Football League along with Midland club Mansfield Town while Barrow and Walsall were seeking re-election.

At the Football League AGM in June Walsall received 33 votes, Barrow 25, Carlisle United 12 and Blyth Spartans and Mansfield Town 10 each. Walsall and Barrow were declared re-elected.

If the club were gutted then they didn't show it with the directors stating at their AGM later that month that 'they were in no way disheartened by the failure of their initial application...and intended to keep this object well in front of them in the coming season.' The club had losses of £41 18s with a wage bill of £1,492 and gate receipts coming in at £4,276.

J. Hunton.

Former Red Rose captain –then Shaddongate and Carlisle United player – John Hunton, who made his debut aged 16 in 1895. Hunton was described as the 'life and soul of the 'unlucky' Rose forward line' and was a speedy dribbler with an effective shot.

19. THE FOOTBALL LEAGUE

UNITED'S FIRST APPLICATION to join the Football League had been submitted during a time of great turmoil with the country rocked by a ten day General Strike from the 3rd to the 13th of May 1926. The deadline for applications had been the on the 7th, right in the middle of national action called by the TUC.

The strike began in defence of miner's wages and hours but soon drew in the railwaymen, transport workers, printers, dockers, ironworkers and steelworkers, so supporters of every side in the NEL from Workington eastwards were affected by it.

Carlisle was solidly out and the city's railway workers were so aggrieved at the methods being used by the bosses following their re-instatement at the return to work that they were urging another national strike by the 18th with only a small proportion of the men that had been called back on shift doing so.

The NEL was expanded by incorporating the

Northern Alliance as a Second Division and Carlisle strengthened their resolve to bring League football to the City by taking on a new trainer, John Hetherington from Ashington, who would regularly put the players through their paces apart from keeper Hood, Smiles and Chambers, who lived and trained outside Carlisle. The local players that re-signed included Ward, Hamilton and Cooper while new players coming in were G. Harrison from Darlington, George Graham from Newcastle, W. Pigg from Ashington and Joseph Reed from Stockport County.

Pigg missed a penalty in a 4-1 opening day defeat at West Stanley that no doubt deflated expectations somewhat and after a customary slow start the *Lancashire Evening Post* was noting that 'there was certainly time for (United) to make their mark, but for an organisation who aim at participating in higher class football (they) should have more than two points from their games.'

The early results may have been disappointing but the form of one new player in particular wasn't and hot-shot centre-forward Jimmy Shankly, who 'possessed a left foot drive of truly awful power,' hit seven during an 11-2 drubbing of Seaton Delaval at Brunton Park. The Scotsman, who had formerly been with Nithsdale, was again instrumental as United stormed back from 2-0 down at half time at fellow League hopefuls Blyth Spartan's Croft Park to win a thriller 5-3.

The club published the following line up for a trip to South Shields reserves a week or two later: Hood; Smiles, Reid; Harrison, Chambers, Pigg (W); Hamilton, Pigg (A), Shankley (with an 'e' thus causing some confusion), Ward and Graham - but his form had attracted the attention of bigger clubs and Shankly did not appear as he was transferred to Sheffield

United on the eve of the game. He had hit 14 goals since joining Carlisle – the highest individual score return in the NEL so far that term.

Jimmy was an older brother of the legendary Bill Shankly who would, of course, play for and manage United himself before his fantastic achievements at Liverpool and William Blyth – almost certainly the Billy Blyth that had captained United before the War and was later a director of the club – was their maternal uncle.

Carlisle were again exempted until the fourth qualifying round of the FA Cup and reached the first round proper by disposing of Whitehaven Athletic at Brunton Park and the directors, who picked the team in those days, were delighted when United dumped out Division Three (North) side Hartlepools United in the first round. 7,000 spectators roared on as the sides came onto the pitch to the strains of the hunting song 'John Peel' being played by a band and 'Pools went ahead in the 20th minute as Robinson beat Hood from close range but United hit back within a minute as Sinclair 'headed a beautiful goal amidst tremendous excitement.' The cheers had barely died down when Albert Pigg 'rushed the ball past Hartlepools' goalkeeper' for number two and just three minutes later Ward added a third following a brilliant individual run.

The second round handed Carlisle an excellent home draw against fellow NEL side Bedlington United and the Blues swept into round three with Smiles netting the first from a penalty before Albert Pigg struck twice in the second half and Smiles was successful with another spot kick in front of 8,000.

The excitement in the City was palpable as the Blues were drawn at home to Wolverhampton Wanderers in the third round. Wolves were a League

Division Two side and they'd beaten Barnsley 9-1 and Bradford City 7-2 already that season.

United may have hoped that the atrocious conditions may have helped them as it rained incessantly during the match and the pitch was churned up – as it happened, the Midlanders were just too good. Wolves went ahead in the 25th minute as Harrington raced through and drew keeper Hood off his line before slipping to Lees, who headed into the empty net. Hood slipped in the mud while trying to recover a back-pass and was punished as Weaver was on it in a flash to put away number two. Carlisle were out but by no means disgraced and, no doubt buoyed by the massive 15,000 crowd that had turned out, in late January the club decided to apply again for the Third Division of the League. The Blues had only been beaten once in the NEL since the beginning of October and had beaten all of the leading sides in the competition, so fancied their chances this time around. The club had taken out a bank overdraft of £560 at the start of the season and despite spending £200 on further ground improvements had a balance of £200.

United had always been 'considered to be one of the NEL's attractive sides' and they looked to press their claim for a League spot by saying that they were accessible by rail, had an average gate of 5,000 spectators in the North Eastern League 'which demonstrated a possibility of 10,000 attendances (in League football) from a town of 50,000 inhabitants, which also taps the districts fond of Association football in East Cumberland.' The Blues finished the season in fifth spot for a second successive time with only the Football League teams reserve sides above them but they'd smashed in 106 goals as they won 23 and drew three of their 38 games.

Rival bidders Mansfield Town were very optimistic at their chances of getting in as they faced up against United, while Blyth Spartans and Chorley were also weighing up their options to get into the League. York City joined the race by sending in an application.

The Northern Clubs in the League didn't show much favour at a meeting held in Manchester when gave a vote of confidence for the two clubs re-applying for admission – Accrington Stanley (19) and Barrow (15) with Carlisle and Mansfield just receiving two votes each, but United pressed ahead to go to the AGM of the English Football League confident that they were 'already assured of considerable support from leading clubs.' The League vote came out as follows: Accrington Stanley 36, Barrow 30, Mansfield 8, York City 6, Carlisle United 5 and Blyth Spartans 3.

Club Chairman Mr. Nicholson said at the club's AGM that applicants to the League weren't fairly treated and weren't given any opportunity to state their case, saying that it seemed to him very unfair that the bottom clubs should be re-elected year after year. But he pointed out that Carlisle United were going to persevere with their application until they gained admission.

The club began strengthening their position for 1927/28 by signing former Newcastle United reserve forward Jack Dowsey from West Ham and goalkeeper Prout from Grimsby Town.

A 3-0 win over Annfield Plain got United away to a good start and a 6-1 demolition job on Hartlepools United reserves fully displayed the Blues' intentions for the season. Carlisle visited Victoria Park for the return in mid-week but were beaten 6-2 with the goals coming during a devastating six minute second half spell. Carlisle had four reserves in the side replacing the backs McQueen and Smiles, the outside-left

Graham and inside-left Ward. Carlisle United: Prout; Fleming and Wilson; Harrison, Ross and Pigg; Bell, Dowsey, Jepson, Cooper and McClusky. Bell scored both goals and Jepson saw a shot hit the bar and go over.

By the end of the month Bedlington United had won their first brace of points in six attempts by beating Carlisle, with the only goal coming from the penalty spot, and the Blues had to 'fight desperately hard to save a point' at Blyth Spartans but inflicted a first defeat on Middlesbrough reserves with Dowsey hitting a hat-trick. Jepson got the other two in a 5-3 success that set Carlisle up nicely for an FA Cup fourth qualifying round tie at Lancaster Town which they won 2-0.

The Blues were drawn against Division Three (North) leaders Doncaster Rovers at Brunton Park in the first round proper and went through 2-1 in a thriller that was described in the press as 'the surprise of the round.' After a period of sustained Carlisle 'bombardment', Ward fired them in front when he gave the Rovers keeper no chance with a powerful drive. McConnell equaliser with a low shot before half time but United regained the advantage when Bell had a shot handled in the area and Jepson stepped up 'to send the ball like lightening into the rigging amid a thunder of applause.'

He almost added his send late on but shot against the bar with a terrific drive and Doncaster had a great chance to take the game to a replay when they themselves were awarded a penalty in the last minute – Proust saving T. Keetley's kick magnificently.

If the Blues were looking to impress the big wigs in charge at the League, then they were going about it in the right way and were handed a big lifeline by Durham City around the time. United's prize for beating Rovers was a second round game against the winners of the City and Wrexham replay, with the Welshmen winning 4-0. Just a few days later it was reported in the Shields Daily News that Carlisle would be invited to take over Durham City's fixtures in the Third Division (North) if the struggling club decided to discontinue their membership. United were prepared to accept the invitation (probably rubbing their hands together at the prospect!) and a strengthened reserve team would continue in the NEL.

United travelled down to the Racecourse Ground and although they were knocked out 'proved that their defeat of section leaders Doncaster was no fluke, and that they have solid grounds for aiming to enter the Northern section,' as reported the *Athletic News*.

8,000 saw United beaten by the only goal scored by Cecil Smith in the 66th minute but they'd hit the bar through Ross earlier. United's final North Eastern League side in the FA Cup was: Prout; Smiles, McQueen; Harrison, Ross, Pigg; Bell, Dowsey, Jepson, Ward and Graham.

Jack Dowsey was transferred to Sunderland soon after for £125, but West Ham held the League transfer and would be pocketing the cash, and clubs from both sides of the border were showing an interest in Pigg, whose brother had gone to Raith Rovers during the summer. The 'Boro were said to be taking a keen interest in his progress.

Prout, Ward and Jepson, who got both goals, impressed in a 'clever' Carlisle side's 2-1 win at Annfield Plain and by the end of March the club had submitted a third application to join the Football League Third Division (North).

The *Star Green 'Un* reckoned the club had 'enjoyed a most successful season from the financial as well as the playing point of view, and believe they would have no difficulty in carrying out their obligations if they were admitted to the League.'

The season turned out to be United's best in the NEL since they'd been Champions; they won 25 of their 38 games and drew 5 to finish runners-up to Sunderland reserves, with the 111 goals that they smashed in proving the club's biggest haul yet.

York City were the next to apply for the Northern section, with some considerable interest being stirred by an amateur team called Argonauts applying for the South section along with Aberdare (who'd knocked United out of the Cup a few seasons back) and Kettering Town.

United captain Robert Ross, who hailed from Falkirk, married a Carlisle lass at Gretna Green on a Saturday morning in front of a fair crowd – and he turned out in front of a bigger one when he played in United's game in the afternoon!

The Blues skipper must have had another broad grin on his face when the Northern Clubs this time came out in support of United's league bid. Nelson were seeking re-election and received 20 votes; the clubs weren't sure if Durham City would have to re-apply at the time, but still came out in favour of United with ten votes to Durham's seven. York City received three and in the event of Barrow having to re-apply, the voting went: Nelson 20, Barrow 16, Carlisle United 2 and York City 2, so United's directors must have been willing their South Cumbrian neighbours to finish strongly.

They did, and finished 19th, 2 points ahead of second-bottom Durham and five ahead of bottom side Nelson.

At the AGM of the Football League at London in June, Nelson received 37 votes and were re-elected. Carlisle United got 33, Durham 11, York City 7 and

Chester 2. The Blues had done it at the third attempt. They were elected members of the Football League Third Division (North) for 1928/29 at old NEL colleagues Durham City's expense. It was quite an achievement for a club from the beyond the mountains in the far north-west that was virtually in Scotland and had started out with no kits, no boots, no ball and not even a pitch.

In fact, when note was made of their Shaddongate history in a newspaper report at the time, they missed out six years of the club's history – and almost 25 years of Carlisle's early football development. The Yorkshire Post wrote that 'A Carlisle football team known as Shaddongate United, a quarter of a century ago, was ambitious and played friendly matches with Lancashire, Northumberland and Durham clubs of good standing. These clubs made the suggestion that Carlisle United would be a name which would have a better gate-drawing power. The suggestion met with favour and at the close of the 1903/04 season the name was changed.'

The same report confirmed that United had bought the Brunton Park ground for £2,000 when they became a limited company in 1921 and that they 'admitted they'd made a big mistake when they did not apply for membership of the Third Division when the Northern Section was formed.'

Red Rose, the City Association, Shaddongate United, the early struggles to establish the game in Carlisle were all consigned to memory and sketchy details that get forgotten and warped over time. Yet some of the 'Gate players will surely have been around to see Carlisle United take their place in the Football League; in their fifties or sixties, suited and dignified with moustaches and hair swept back with the new Brylcreem pomade run through their combs, watching on silently from the stand; their ghosts now prowling the turf in greying flickers.

There isn't even much ephemera around relating to the 'Gate. Match programmes are a real rarity and Victorian supporter's cards don't appear featuring the side very often, if ever. There are no old black and white film clips of Shaddongate United in action. Just a few newspaper clippings and maybe an old silver medal or two, the engravings on the back worn smooth by generations of fingers, that no doubt lie about in dusty, forgotten drawers in the City.

During the first season in Division Three a Yorkshire newspaper reporter dubbed United 'the club that killed rugby in Carlisle.' The Association game had won out in the end.

We are Shaddongate.

Our ball is round.

RANGERS AT CARLISLE.

The Rangers, led by Spencer, taking the field at Carlisle on Saturday.

McConnell, the Carlisle centre forward, scoring the fourth goal after eluding Mul keen, who ran out and who is here seen sprawling on the ground.
"Courier" Photos.

Glasgow Rangers at Brunton Park in 1930.

Site of the former Red Rose pitch at Maryport Cottages and below, looking across the Caldew at the pitch from Holme Head.

Site of Shaddongate United's Willowholme pitch today.

ABOUT THE AUTHOR

Jon Tait was born in Ashington, Northumberland in 1972. He is a freelance writer and was the press officer at both Gretna Football Club and the Northern Football Alliance. He has a degree in Journalism and spent ten years covering Carlisle United as an agency reporter for the national press. He has written a number of books and works part-time as a postman.

Printed in Great Britain
by Amazon